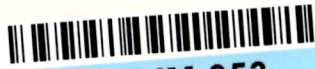

THE FUTURE OF SCOTLAND

The Future of Scotland

EDITED BY ROBERT UNDERWOOD

CROOM HELM LONDON

©1977 The Nevis Institute
Croom Helm Ltd, 2-10 St John's Road, London SW11

British Library Cataloguing in Publication Data

The future of Scotland.
   1. Scotland — Social conditions
   I. Underwood, Robert
   309. 1'411'0857   HN398.S3

ISBN 0-85664-476-5 hardback
ISBN 0-85664-695-4 paperback

Printed in Great Britain 78- 3876
by Redwood Burn Ltd, Trowbridge and Esher

CONTENTS

CONTRIBUTORS

Robert Underwood Director of the Nevis Institute

Christopher Smout Professor of Economic History at the University of Edinburgh

George Bruce poet and critic, is currently Visiting Professor of English at Wooster College, Ohio

Donald Duff Professor of Applied Geology at Strathclyde University

John Francis at the time of writing was Senior Research Fellow in Energy Studies at Heriot-Watt University

Kenneth Blaxter FRS Director of the Rowett Research Institute, Aberdeen

Michael Parry Secretary to the Scottish Council for Postgraduate Medical Education

James Scotland CBE Principal of Aberdeen College of Education and Chairman of the General Teaching Council for Scotland

Andrew Hargrave freelance financial and industrial journalist

John Evans formerly Director of the Scottish Council Research Institute

Olaf Thornton Convenor of a transport study group for the Scottish Council for Development and Industry; he was formerly Managing Director of Rolls Royce in Scotland

Jan Fladmark Assistant Director of the Countryside Commission for Scotland and Honorary Fellow, University of Edinburgh

John Erickson Professor of Politics and Director of Defence Studies Unit at the University of Edinburgh

James Kellas Senior Lecturer in Politics at Glasgow University

William Robertson CBE Executive Vice-President of the Scottish Council for Development and Industry

INTRODUCTION

Industrial society has developed by separating into well defined specialities both the tasks of everyday life and its knowledge. But now, dependent upon that specialisation, it faces complex and serious issues whose resolution demands an understanding of their interactions, for which academics as much as business people are ill prepared.

The Nevis Institute has been founded to stimulate and to develop a clearer view of the connections between different disciplines. It believes that only with such an improved understanding can credible anticipations for the future be formed. Whilst maintaining a world perspective of the issues which it studies, it intends to bring them to a Scottish focus. It does this not from narcissistic parochialism but simply in the hope of achieving a sensible scale for the study and resolution of problems. Scotland and the northern islands have an historic identity which permits their separate study, but are sufficiently important in their involvement with world affairs to give a wider relevance to the work produced by the Nevis Institute.

This, the first book of the Institute, is intended to provide a frame work for conjecture. Scotland shares the problems of all western socie-ies, but geography and industrial history have given them a special character. It is the task of this book to describe these special characteristics and to set the issues that shape them in a world context. The unbiased, detached view taken by the book is offered as an informed contribution to the wide ranging reappraisal of Scottish identity and world position currently being debated.

These essays are based upon the lectures given in the series 'Scotland and the Future' which was sponsored by the University of Edinburgh's School of the Man Made Future, which has since been closed. That series and associated projects, which were conducted during the first half of 1976, highlighted the need for the establishment of an independent body to be concerned with issues related to the future in Scotland. The Nevis Institute has been founded to serve that need.

Anticipations derive from the fusion of understanding gained from past experiences, with the appreciation of current circumstances. The different views of the future come from different interpretations. Those whose job is to make preparations for the future need images and concepts of the future. Frequently these models of what the future holds are different for each expert group; they are usually assumed and not stated.

The Institute works with trans-disciplinary groups who address particular issues or problems. These groups of experts, who usually do not work together, need to make their assumptions explicit in order to develop an agreed working basis. This process of linking together people with different assumptions will in itself be beneficial. But additionally those associated with the Institute expect to improve their insights of future possibilities enabling them to be better prepared for the way ahead.

Christopher Smout and George Bruce open with their varying inter-pretations of Scottish Identity. In the context of resources, minerals, energy and food are considered, while human potential is discussed with reference to health, education, enterprise and economics. With the basic scene set attention turns to some of the issues of strategic planning, transport, building and defence. Finally, James Kellas looks at Scotland's political system and the ways in which it is likely to respond to changes.

This book reflects not only the work of the contributors and those others who have directly assisted in its compilation, but also those formerly involved with the School of the Man Made Future and those people who have contributed to the founding of the Nevis Institute. Thanks are extended to all of these people. The contributors write as individuals and not as representatives of the organisations or bodies with which they are associated. Nor does this book put forward a common interpretation, rather its approach to some aspects of the situation reflects a plurality of thinking. And these differences are as important as the areas of agreement in catalysing thought and action for the long term future in Scotland.

Edinburgh   Robert Underwood
February 1977

1 THE SCOTTISH IDENTITY

Christopher Smout

There may be a Scottish identity, which is the heritage of the Scottish past, but there is no Scottish people in a racial sense. Early medieval Scotland was a peculiar amalgam of Picts, Irish Celts, Vikings, Britons, Angles, Normans and Flemings. In the course of hundreds of years these people and tribes became fused into a nation state, though with at least three strong regional identities, that of the highlands, of the lowlands and of the northern isles. Then industrialisation and a quarter of a millenium of union with the rest of Britain had its effect. Many Scots today are descended from very recent immigrants. About one in six are catholics, and most of these are descended from the Irish peasantry of Victoria's reign.

In the 1961 census of Scotland nearly a quarter of a million people were reported as born in England and Wales, which is a larger absolute number (though representing a much smaller proportion of the population) than the maximum number of Irish-born reported in any of the decennial nineteenth century censuses. Then there are the Poles, the Jews, the Italians, the Pakistanis, the Americans, all immigrants in small numbers, but all with the right and opportunity to be or to become as Scottish as the next man. To live in Scotland with the consciousness of being Scottish does not imply the same spiritual and material goals as the followers of Robert I or of Prince Charles Edward Stuart. Scotland is part of the modern, agnostic, consumer, capitalist society, facing problems of resource shortage, and potential nuclear extinction. That society is the West.

The history of the Union enshrines the continuing central paradox of the Scottish identity. It bears witness to the survival of an elemental nationalist consciousness that Scotland is not England; and on the other hand it carries the apparently opposing consciousness that Scotland and England are linked within a national British entity. Whether the union breaks up next year, or continues forever, the highly complex feelings that Scots have had for hundreds of years about their relationship to the English are unlikely to change overnight.

The Union of the Crowns in 1603 was the moment when dynastic accident first led to the compromising of Scotland's independence. There was then one King and two governments, with the Scottish government generally a satellite of the will of a London resident King. On several

important occasions in the seventeenth century, those who might be
said to speak for Scotland (Churchmen, merchants, the whole convention
of the States on one occasion) strove for an even closer political union
with England. Yet in the same century there was a national rebellion
because one King tried to impose an English-type liturgy on the Scottish
church, and later extensive anti-English demonstrations at the time of
the Darien scheme because another tried to prevent the Scots setting up
a colony in territory claimed by the King of Spain. The ambivalent
character of Scottish feelings towards England was thus evident at a
very early date in the modern period, but it is worth noticing that no
explicitly nationalist movement ever appeared in the seventeenth century, and no unionist one either. The struggles were about religion,
dynastic power, and trade; attitudes towards England were taken up in
relation to these questions, not in relation to the concept of the nation
as such.

Since the formal Union of Parliaments in 1707 Anglo-Scottish relations have gone through several further stages. The Union itself was
urged by England, whose earlier indifference to closer relations suddenly
changed when the Scots threatened to choose a different successor to
Queen Anne. England feared that the ending of the Union of the Crowns
would lead to a revival of the old Scottish/French Alliance, and therefore
to an intolerable security threat. It was accepted by the Scots parliament
for complex reasons that have been the cause of much discussion. The
economic and political arguments against going it alone were very strong,
but the Ministry at Westminster did not hesitate to use the gum of patronage and bribery to secure its friends to the side of what contemporaries
called an incorporating union. Perhaps the most interesting thing about
1707, however, is that it was not an incorporating union at all. The
Scottish church was left intact; the Scottish legal profession was left
quite separate; the Royal burghs, their merchants and tradesmen, were
left in possession of their ancient privileges. In these ways the economic
interests and career structures of those whom we would now term the
Scottish middle classes were entirely secured from English encroachment.
Scottish education and Scottish Poor Law developed unhindered taking
a radically different direction from their English equivalents. All that was
incorporated was parliament, and eighteenth-century parliaments did
much less, and mattered much less in the lives of ordinary people than
parliaments do today. Certainly union, once achieved, was accepted without enthusiasm or complaint by the majority of Scots, in much the same
way as entering the EEC has been accepted in Britain in the last two
years.

To this there are two exceptions. Firstly, the majority of the gentry and polite intelligentsia of the eighteenth century appear to have been enthusiastic unionists and anglophiles, although capable on occasion of powerful outbreaks of Scotch anger if like Boswell in London they felt their nation was being slighted by the Sassenach. Secondly, in the first half of the eighteenth century there were the Jacobites who wished to overthrow the Hanoverian State, to assert the excellence of older and more Scottish ways. It is doubtful that they were nationalists in any simple sense, as the Stuart Pretenders themselves wanted to reign in London and not in Edinburgh, and certainly they had little following, as the failure of their plots and risings in 1708, 1715, 1719 and 1745 all showed. Thereafter there was within the eighteenth century no opposition to the Union as such.

No doubt the eighteenth-century Union was the more acceptable because from about 1740 it began to benefit the economy in a very clear and unequivocal way for Scotland. There is no evidence from 1707 to about 1740 that it made much difference either way, but thereafter there were three main directions of growth. Firstly, there was the growing prosperity of the pastoral farmers now able to sell more and more cattle to the English market as the price for meat rose in the south. Secondly, there was the rise of Glasgow in the tobacco trade, something which could not possibly have occurred unless Scotland with Virginia and Maryland had been part of the same Empire. Thirdly, and most important, there was the growth of the linen industry. As early as 1760 perhaps one Scottish family in four or five drew some income from it. Up to a third of the linen woven was at times directed to markets in the West Indies or in the thirteen colonies of North America; perhaps another third was sold in England, and a larger quantity of yarn was sold annually to Lancashire manufacturers. It is little wonder that the connection with England was cherished by some and tolerated by virtually all in the eighteenth century. There has never been a period when there is so little doubt that it worked strongly to Scotland's material advantage.

Scotland continued to flourish exceedingly within the framework of the Union in the nineteenth century. A free-trade Britain that was the workshop of the world was an excellent environment for a Scotland which exported a high proportion of her manufactured goods. The first manifestation of the Industrial Revolution in Scotland was the growth of the cotton industry, its easy transplantation from Lancashire to Scotland being itself a fruit of the Union. The growth of the iron industry in early Victorian times was more firmly set on the exploitation of Scot-

land's own natural resources, but owed a lot on the demand side to the
industrialisation of other parts of Britain. The rise of the Clyde as a ship-
building centre, also rested partly on Scottish resources and partly on
external demand. The quite extraordinary success of the West of Scotland
meant that this area was largely exempted from very serious signs of
industrial lag that began to appear in the closing part of the nineteenth
century in many other parts of Britain.

All the indications are that in the second half of the nineteenth century, Scotland, through industrialisation, gained rapidly in wealth and
income compared to the rest of Britain. She was, of course, still much
poorer than England as late as the middle of the nineteenth century,
though by then the extreme disparities of the Union were being narrowed.
The north of Scotland remained poorer throughout the period down to
the first world war; but farm incomes (the main form of income in this
area) drew within four per cent of the national British average. The south
(i.e. south of the industrial belt) was a relatively high income area in
terms of farm wages, again its main occupation, from the 1860s onwards.
But the real success story was in the central belt, where increasingly the
population came to concentrate. In 1850 this had been a low wage
region, and one of the attractions for capitalists moving to Scotland was
probably that wages were well below the national British average. By the
1880s it had achieved parity with the British average; by the early twentieth century it was one of the four highest (out of thirteen) wage regions
into which Britain has been divided by scholars. It is worth remembering
that industrialisation for all its cost in terms of eviction, slums and displacement, brought higher incomes to the working classes, as it did to
every other rank in society. So far as union with England was the framework within which this industrialisation occurred, it was as acceptable
as the greater prosperity itself.

Nevertheless, the nineteenth century also saw a very significant shift
in the role of Westminster within Scotland, and this began to give an
entirely new political dimension to the Union. Reform Bills from 1832
onwards progressively created a new Scottish electorate, ultimately a
fairly democratic one, in place of the handful of lairds and their creat-
ures who had chosen MPs in the eighteenth century. It meant that political participation by the majority of Scots began to become possible.
The problems of the Victorian state became so enormous that the government had to interfere in the way that Scottish local authorities did (or
more often failed to do) their duty. Thus statutes emanating from Westminster altered the framework of the Scottish Poor Law in 1845, of the
Scottish school system in 1872, and by a whole series of statutes local

authorities were stimulated, or bullied, to tackle the problems of public health and housing in the burgeoning and cholera-ridden cities.

Westminster behaved towards Scotland in the nineteenth century with ineptness balanced by modesty, a combination that simultaneously aroused and assuaged Scottish ire. Several of the early statutes with major affects on Scotland were incompetently drafted because parliament took insufficient trouble to inform itself about the peculiarities of the Scottish situation. This, along with minor irritations caused by the insensitiveness of England to Scotland's habits and usages, led in 1853 to the National Association for the Vindication of Scottish Rights. This romantic but briefly very popular protonationalist body was devoted not to breaking up the Union, but to reasserting the distinctiveness of Scotland within it. It was the tip of an iceberg of public opinion to whom Scotland was not England despite the prosperity and general acceptability of the Union. After this date Scotland always had a small but vociferous lobby ready to claim that the spirit or letter of the Union had been breached by English highhandedness.

But the Victorian state, still diffident in any case at the prospect of government interference and wedded to laissez-faire theory, ultimately reacted sensibly in the face of Scottish sensitivity. It did not try to establish a British poor law or a British School Board system, but it set up bodies in Edinburgh to administer the reformed Scottish systems. When it reformed crofting tenures in the 1880s, other new bodies, the Land Court and the Crofters' Commission, were set up in Scotland, and finally, in 1885, it bowed to mounting public pressure and established a Scottish Secretary of State. In the context of Victorian Britain this seemed to be as much devolution as public opinion demanded: it maintained the identity of Scotland as part of Britain and at the same time as distinct from England. The Victorians had an instinct for this outside the sphere of politics; they founded a Scottish football association, not a British one, and a Scottish TUC that had ties to the British one, but which was not identical to it.

The twentieth century, however, was quite different in important ways from the two preceding ones. First of all the economic situation was relatively less favourable. Although the national income of Britain continued to rise quite rapidly, and that of Scotland to rise with it, until average incomes and affluences were considerably above what they had been in 1900, the relative position of Scotland probably slipped somewhat. In 1974 Scotland as a whole lay sixth out of the nine wage regions into which the country was divided. Although by 1975, under the influence of the oil boom, she had improved her place in this league table to third, this very recent development is quite untypical of the twentieth century trend. In 1964 for example, the average earnings of the Scottish male were 8.4 per cent below the UK average. Furthermore the twentieth century Scottish economy has suffered from prolonged and peculiar problems, especially in the west central belt that had been the apex of Victorian prosperity. The dreadful experience of unemployment in heavy industries between the wars is the most obvious example and the failure of the region to reconstruct and diversify its economy sufficiently after the second world war was equally important. Even during the prosperous 1960s the average rate of unemployment in Scotland was twice that of the UK as a whole. Nor should it be overlooked that the dissolution of the British Empire closed the door for countless Scots who had gone adventuring as administrators, soldiers, or just as emigrants, from the middle of the eighteenth century until the inter-war years.

Whereas up to the first world war almost all firms operating within Scotland were controlled from Scotland, thereafter more and more people found themselves the employees of State-run enterprises, or of firms based in London or abroad. Many Scots have bitterly resented the challenge to the control of their own economy A threat that never existed even in the Industrial Revolution, or the prosperity of high Victorian times, simply because before the days of modern communications it was impossible to run a business from hundreds of miles away. They see in the Union an obstacle to Scotsmen successfully reasserting control over their own lives. There may be much truth in their view. But few emphasise that remote control is also a European phenomenon, and perhaps the inescapable concomitant of a mixed economy and the rise of multi-national corporations. Nor is it easy to discover any recipe for unscrambling multi-national eggs.

The other dominant theme of the twentieth century has been the continuing enlargement of the sphere of the state in everyday life, with until recently, growing insensitivity on the part of that state to local considerations, or perhaps a growing confidence on the part of an increasingly professional bureaucracy that they know best. Thus the Scottish Poor Law was ultimately replaced by the British Welfare State, and the finance of Scottish Universities was funnelled through a British University Grants Commission. There are quite good arguments in terms of efficiency for doing these things, but it is perilous in a society which is still deeply conscious that Scotland is not England, and fairly determined to keep things that way. In the twentieth century, therefore, the Union has suddenly begun to take on an incorporative nature that it never had in the past. Politically, however, virtually no steps have been taken yet to counteract these basic shifts, and since Scotland has in no way lost its consciousness of wishing to maintain its difference from England it is not in the least surprising that a Scottish National Party dedicated to breaking off the Union should have grown from a small, sectarian, and cranky base, in the years before the second world war, into a powerful political movement.

Suppose that within the next ten years Scotland will obtain sufficient devolution or independence to manage her own affairs in some meaningful way. Further suppose that the road of human choice forks again, one sign says 'this way to a growth economy, maximise your economic opportunities and visit us'. The other sign says 'this way to a no-growth economy, conserve your dwindling resources and visit us'. When politicians talk about the future of Scotland, it is often described in terms of a trip to maxi-growth land, and in their travel brochures the national Volkswagen is usually parked in a landscape like that of Scandinavia. The reasoning seems to go like this; Scotland is a small northern nation and wants self-government; Denmark, Norway and Sweden are small northern nations, and they enjoy self-government; given self-government, or at least meaningful devolution, Scandinavian prosperity can be recreated in Scotland. But not all small independent northern European countries are prosperous: Eire might be a more likely version of Scotland's future.

Sweden is blessed by abundant resources of timber and iron ore on which she raised herself to prosperity in the nineteenth century and which have helped to sustain her prosperity in the twentieth century until she has become the wealthiest country in the Western world. Scotland plus or minus oil could not match that. On the other hand Denmark is much worse off than Scotland in terms of natural resources, lacking minerals and having very indifferent agricultural land, despite her fame as an exporter of farming produce. What does Denmark have which Scotland does not have? In a nutshell the answer is very much higher productivity. And the reason for this seems to be rooted in a Scandinavian attitude of mind that could be described as co-operative, innovative and flexible, whereas Scots tend to be suspicious of one another, conservative and inflexible. These differences are not due to race, or even primarily to the fact that Scotland is not a self-governing country, but are rooted in the historical experiences of the societies concerned.

A hundred years ago the majority of Scandinavians were peasants who owned their own land, who were in a relatively egalitarian society in their country villages, and who were accustomed to a wide degree of co-operation between one another in their farming operations. Rapid economic growth then took place, in Denmark on the basis of the export of their agricultural goods to Britain and Germany, largely made possible by the development of Producers' Co-operatives, and subsequently the basis of industrialisation mainly through light industries and the small firm. The story in Sweden (and Norway) also emphasises the importance of primary products in the early days and of manufactured goods later, though in Sweden in particular the firms were quite large. Simultaneously there was political revolution, so that by the first world war all three countries had peacefully become modern democracies. In this extremely rapid and even transformation the fabric of society was never torn, everyone's income went up so fast that there was general agreement that economic change under capitalism was a good thing. Power passed to the people so smoothly that they never lost the sense that government was something for which they were responsible. The state was theirs, not the prerogative of some other governing class, and in each country great importance was laid upon universal and excellent education that would train the Scandinavian not merely for work and competition (although they did do that) but also for citizenship. In essence these are three highly successful modern societies which have kept a tradition of consensus, of mutual help, of working to a common purpose, and of welcoming change and novelty for the opportunities which it may bring.

Scotland, by contrast, has a seriously damaged social fabric. The experience of the Scottish working class has not historically been that economic change under capitalism was always a good thing. Despite the benefits referred to, economic change in the nineteenth century swept thousands into the lowland cities out of Ireland and out of the highlands in circumstances where the push of eviction or economic collapse was often much stronger than the pull of high wages. Economic change likewise created the disastrous levels of unemployment of the inter-war years, with their apparently ineradicable consequences of Union suspicion of labour-saving techniques that they have left behind. More generally Scandinavian society did not allow such exploitive relationships as British society.

On the political front the Scottish working man has never felt that the State was in any sense his own, partly perhaps because of the absence of Home Rule, but also because of the persistence of the dishonest franchise system and the persistence of a British ruling class that has continued to keep its hands on the levers of power. And lastly, the Scottish working class and middle class alike has been exposed for a century to a miserable education system (Scottish run, too) which believes that teaching consists of trying to smash facts into children. How can constructive consensus, adventure and innovation be produced in a society where phalanges of silent children arrive at the universities with their pens poised to catch truth as it drips from their teachers' lips? Scandinavian society is the product of Scandinavian history, and to reproduce it in Scotland requires overcoming an historical inheritance of industrial paranoia, alienation from the State, and bad schools. It would need to be done deliberately and would take time. There is some danger that it might not be done at all, because the imperfection of past practice may be mistaken for some kind of 'Scottish tradition' that has to be kept in being.

Finally, imagine that in the course of the next century the prophecies of the doomwatch come to pass, that the world's natural resources are seriously depleted and that nothing is found to replace them. Imagine that it has become necessary in the West to put up with nil or even declining economic growth, not just in the odd years of a depression, but in the long term.

In these circumstances could Scotland be the very world leader at achieving a harmonious society with negative growth? The basis for a no-growth society of this kind must be a sense of contentment and resignation. Requiring either contentment with the levels of social welfare spending already achieved, which means putting up with the slums for ever, or acceptance of a further permanent cut in personal living standards in order to finance slum-clearance. The fatalism demanded by a no-growth society would provide few opportunities for upward social mobility or private enrichment. In fact a declining rather than a stagnant economy need not just contentment and resignation to an even higher degree, but a strong sense of consensus in agreeing what to abandon as real wealth falls. Universities, medicine, private transport, private incomes altogether perhaps? The prospect of doing that peacefully is mind-boggling.

The idea of economic growth as a possible or justifiable aim for a society is comparatively recent in terms of human history. Before about 1500 it was simply not part of man's mental equipment: the enrichment of the West was so slow as to be imperceptible from generation to generation. At first it was assumed that enrichment of one community was at the expense of someone else, and that wealthy states could be made or unmade by the exercise of military force. The notion that a state could by its policies and its armies systematically pursue economic gain for the welfare of its citizens and the glory of its Prince fully arrived with sixteenth and seventeenth century mercantilism, but the realisation that economic growth could be attained even without harming your neighbour by snatching a bigger slice of the cake only arrived with the works of David Hume and Adam Smith in the eighteenth century.

Pre-growth societies were indeed well adjusted to the facts of a no-growth life for their citizens. Resignation, acceptance of an inherited social place that appeared to be divinely sanctioned, respect for a hierarchy where the decisions were always made at the top—these were very deeply engrained by the socialising agencies. But could modern Scottish society return to a parallel frame of mind, or at least attain a version of it that was equally functional, if hopefully more democratic? The greatest obstruction to achieving a happy no-growth society (if that is what we really want) would again be the educational system. Since the advent of growth in the eighteenth century we have been devising socialisation processes that count getting on in the world as the main aim of an individual's life. Beating facts into children may not be a very effective way of promoting economic growth or anything else except anxiety and silence in the young, but when it is combined, as pre-eminently it has been in Scotland since the nineteenth century, with a competitive grading system, it does train the young to believe that the world is an hierarchy of brain, and that those with brains who have swallowed the facts should legitimately get on in the world and become rich. Ever since the eighteenth century, Scottish universities have prided themselves on being open to the working class, but admittance to a Scottish University has also always been a passport into the middle classes, and those who graduate increasingly regard themselves as an élite entitled to higher earnings and more privileges than those who have never been there. The recent great success of interested parties in turning the school teachers' profession into a closed guild for those with degrees, irrespective of their competence at the job, is one telling example of this.

As long as education is treated as a competitive race with high prizes for a limited number of winners, the result will be a society that is spurred on by dissatisfaction, by need for achievement, by absence of resignation and by social ambition. No bad thing, perhaps, for a growth-oriented world, though other emphases might be even more appropriate. But for a happy no-growth world it would not be enough in Scotland, or anywhere in the West, just to make a political decision to go for no-growth. Bringing it about would mean reversing engines on two hundred years of history and to try to make acceptance of one's lot in life and the absence of ambition the qualities rewarded in the family and in the school. Perhaps it could happen on the Isle of Lewis, where pre-industrial values very remarkably survive, but the ordinary Lowland Scot would rather do anything than submit to the indignity of resignation and uncompetitiveness. So how will it all end? A high growth performance will in practice turn out to be extremely difficult, and perhaps impossible. A happy no-growth performance is not feasible. It will end in an ordinary low-growth performance with or without independence, but by some acts of the political will we could nevertheless in some respects make Scotland a better place to be a Scot in.

2 THE ARTS IN SCOTLAND

George Bruce

Is there, it must be asked, any such thing as the Scottish identity? Over forty years ago, Edwin Muir, who coming from Orkney had a detachment from the Scottish scene rarely given to mainland Scots, wrote in his book *Scottish Journey*:

> Scotland is, like all countries, a confusing conglomeration, containing such strange anachronisms as Edinburgh, a great expanse of fallow land, and a number of different races. In the course of my journeyings I came in contact with these various Scotlands, passing from one into another without rhyme or reason, as it seemed to me; but what Scotland is I am still unable to say. It is Edinburgh, certainly, and Airdrie, and Glasgow and Kirriemuir, and the Kailyard, and the rich agricultural areas of the South, and the depopulated glens of Sutherland, and the prosperous island of Orkney. It has a human north and south, east and west, as well as a geographical; but though they have been clamped within a small space for a long time, one feels they have never met. Then there is the rivalry between Edinburgh and Glasgow, ridiculous in essence, jocular in expression and acrid in spirit; there are the various classes, of which I found the working—or rather the workless—class by far the most honestly admirable; there are the Socialists, the intellectuals—mostly anti-Calvanistic, the Fascists, the Nationalists, the hikers and the churchgoers. Finally cutting across the classifications, come the Highlanders and the Lowlanders. No two sets of people could be more temperamentally incompatible.

Edwin Muir's experience casts doubt on the idea of a single Scottish identity, but a journey through England would also have yielded a variety of human characteristics, though these might not have run to the extremities of the Scots. It is unlikely, however, that an English writer would have raised the question of identity. Englishness, whatever that meant, would be taken for granted.

In Scotland it was otherwise with Scottish writers and with many Scots. They tended to assert their differences—from the English especially. The British assertion was felt to be necessary because the English public and government behaved as if Scottish institutions embodying concepts of a distinctive way of life did not exist. Scots Law, the Church of Scotland, and Scottish Education, indicated the existence of an ethos that differed from that underlying similar institutions in England. Scottish education is more democratic than English education, which still sets a high value on the separatist fee-paying, private schools, oddly referred to as Public Schools. Despite the protest implied by the revival of writing in Scots, first in the 1920s and then in a second wave during the forties, a general lack of confidence in the idea of a Scottish culture was evident, not only as might be expected in England, but in the curricula of Scottish schools and universities. At best even until recently, and perhaps even now, Scottish literature and Scottish history were taught as adjuncts to English/British History and English Literature. I recollect a Professor of English Literature in Scotland remarking to a class of students in the early thirties: 'We must admit the culture is south of the Border.' This was not intended as a snub, but as an observation of fact. If there was work of Scottish character of especial merit—and there was, MacDiarmid's early Scots lyrics having been published in the early twenties and his *A Drunk Man Looks at the Thistle* in 1926—its existence had been effectively concealed, even from the Scots themselves. In any case, it was argued by many in authority, MacDiarmid's writings were mannered eccentricities.

The Scots, however, did export an image of themselves which proved very acceptable south of the Border, a variant of which is still successfully promoted on the television screen and on stage. The stage Scot is heavily be-tartaned. Though apparently a highlandman, being dressed in a kilt, he speaks the language of the lowlands, a rugged, hearty speech, with a strong emphasis on the 'r's, fabricated so that it represents no particular locality, and is readily comprehended by Englishmen and Americans. The standard type has run from Harry Lauder to Andy Stewart. Despite the impression that he has been custom-built to meet commercial requirements, he has a history. When Sir Walter Scott persuaded George IV to wear a kilt on the occasion of his visit to Scotland, he was unconsciously, no doubt, preparing a pattern of the distortions of the Highland tradition which has since presumed to represent Scottishness. Another false representation of the Scot, which was regarded as even more truly Scottish was to be found in the writings of the 'Kailyard School', the most distinguished member of which was the playwright, Sir J.M. Barrie. Of the Kailyard School George Blake wrote that it was 'to sentimentalize and popularize a merely vestigial and unrepresentative Scotland'. Unrepresentative the movement may have been, but so successful was its promotion, and so conveniently acceptable was its easy senti-

ment and simple humour that it obscured, and inhibited more genuine
and original developments in the arts in Scotland.

Significantly the feature that was omitted from the kailyard and
stage Scot was intelligence. All too readily the British Council concluded, apparently, that there was too little intelligence in the writings of
Scots to justify their inclusion in their books of appraisal of British poets,
with the exception of Edwin Muir. After long delay, and after the publication of several minor contemporary English poets, Hugh MacDiarmid,
is now on their lists.

In 1922 two literary works were published in Britain which could
be regarded as indices of the conditions of the psyche of England and
Scotland – T.S. Eliot's *The Waste Land* and Hugh MacDiarmid's maga-
zine *The Scottish Chapbook.* Eliot's poem with its flat rhythms and sense
of anxiety, its 'fragments shored against my ruins' amounted to a poetic
statement of the collapse of the traditional cultures and faiths in urban
societies. When I first read the poem in 1929 or 1930, it seemed to me
to apply as exactly to urban Scotland (and three-quarters of the people
of Scotland lived in the urbanised area of the Central Lowlands), as it
did to England. It was a pointer to the decivilisation, evidence of which
is to be seen in the commercialised pop cultures which spread anon-
ymously throughout Europe and America, and in the ready acceptance
of violence as a solution to personal and sometimes national frustrations.
The effect of the destruction of the continuity of traditional modes of
living which till recently were found capable of modification to meet
changing conditions and of the rejection of social responsibility, is to
be seen in the 'opting out' of increasing numbers of the young by drug
taking, and other devices of withdrawal. The final condition of this withdrawal has been prophesied in *The Private Future* by Martin Pawley, the
last paragraph of which concludes:

> . . . alone in a centrally heated air-conditioned capsule, drugged, fed
> with music and erotic imagery, the parts of his consciousness separ-
> ated into components that reach everywhere and nowhere, the private
> citizen of the future will have become one with the end of effort and
> the triumph of sensation divorced from action. When the barbarians
> arrive they will find him like some ancient Greek sage, lost in con-
> templation, terrified and yet fearless, listening to himself.

This sounds rather melodramatic and oversimplified to carry conviction,
but it relates to the tone of the more concerned recent drama. Harold
Pinter's plays are frequently about people enclosed in a room. Outside

in the cold there is an undefined threat. He described the situation in an interview thus:

> Outside the room is a world bearing down upon them, which is frightening. We are all in this, all in a room, and outside is a world . . . which is most inexplicable, and frightening, curious and alarming.

Other modern literature confirms the conclusion that modern man lives in a world which is increasingly meaningless to him. The dramatist Ionesco, described the condition: 'Cut off from his religious, metaphysical and transcendental roots man is lost, all his actions become senseless, absurd and useless.' I have taken the quotation from Martin Esslin's book, *Theatre of the Absurd* in which he comments:

> The sense of metaphysical anguish at the absurdity of the human condition is broadly speaking the theme of the plays of Beckett, Ionesco, Genet and the other writers discussed in this book.

What is shared by these writers is the threat of non-entity. Their identity—their sense of the reality of their being—nevertheless depends on their acceptance of the conditions which they see as truth. In *The Myth of Sysphus,* in 1942, Camus wrote of modern, self-conscious man, 'His is an irremediable exile, because he is deprived of the memories of a lost homeland as much as he lacks the hope of a promised life to come.' Thereafter, in his book *The Rebel*, Camus having accepted the inevitable destruction of man in a nonsensical universe, he proceeded to build hope out of despair. Man's enduring courage and the endless spirit of enquiry remains.

To concern oneself with the idea of a Scottish identity when the question which has occupied those writers responsive to the developing intellectual climate over the past hundred years, seems hardly pertinent. In so far as Scottish writers are to be regarded as serious they will participate in these developments. One must, however, ask the question as to whether fictive creations are possible without a 'habitation and a name'. Perhaps the earliest example of awareness of identity under threat as normal is Herman Melville's short story, *Bartleby*. Bartleby is a scrivener who has been employed as a copyist by a lawyer. Left to himself to carry out his routine duties, no complaint can be laid against him, but his employer, wishing to show his interest in his clerk brings him into his office. From that moment Bartleby resists all innovations to his work, with the gentle but firm refusal of 'I prefer not to'. This innocent, but impenitently persistent, man dies in gaol, still reiterating, 'I prefer not to'. About a hundred years later, in 1952, Samuel Beckett's *Waiting for Godot* made its appearance on the stage. Beckett's progression from this play has been marked by his removing from his characters, even those small supports which make life bearable.

Whereas Bartleby's concern was that nothing should happen to him, the two tramps in Beckett's play, are given a purpose by waiting for Godot, whoever he may be. At the end of the play, they are still on the same road, at the same place, still waiting. Only time has changed. On the face of it the audience should feel the emptiness of life, and frustration at unfulfilled hopes, but I suspect that the popularity the play now enjoys is due to the comic identity of the tramps. They belong to a long tradition of clowns or fools. Even if Beckett intended them to be French clowns they have on the English stage assumed the characteristics of the down-and-outs of any place in which they are played, who make a comedy of their plight. They remain affectionately in the memory, as if their creator had given them *his* affection. They are not clowns anonymous. They are particular creations, and their speech echoes with reminders of traditional readings of life. Fragmented and piecemeal as are the references they are themselves whole creations.

The theory of the theatre of the absurd may relate to the universe in which they exist, but they themselves are no abstracts but are textures of experience. On the one hand the vision of the contemporary artist points to the anonymity and isolation of the individual now and in the future, and on the other, those characters who speak out of the conditions which make for non-entity, yet show in their tattered, unhappy selves, individual characters. Even when Sam Shephard, the American playwright, in his play, *Actions*, makes its main characteristic non-communication, there still remains a sense of meaning locked in the person. Unlike the characters in the majority of Pinter's plays the principal characters in *Waiting for Godot* and the four characters in *Actions* have no social status. They are therefore in the classic tragic situation of confronting the gods or the emptiness of nature alone. The tramps in *Waiting for Godot* are less alone than the two shabby men and two shabby women in *Actions* because they share a common language, whereas in *Actions*, even though the period of the play is Christmas, symbolised by a Christmas tree and by the meal being turkey, they are unable to recount the story of Christmas or any story at all. The best they can do is to act. The first significant action occurs when one of the men in frustration at his inability to communicate smashes his chair to pieces. It is as if it were being said if we cannot have love we shall have hate. The four are bound together by sharing food and drink—the drink is water which has to be fetched from a well—by washing and drying dishes and clothes. The fulfilment at this elementary level is matched by the frustration of the inability to speak meaningful words. The situation is reminiscent of the dying mother in Faulkner's story, *As I Lay Dying* who says:

> And so when Cora Tull would tell me I was not a true mother, I would think how words go straight up in a thin line, quick and harmless and how terribly doing goes along the earth, clinging to it, so that after a while the two lines are too far apart for the same person to straddle from one to the other.

The problem of communication was also recognised by Hemingway. In his short story, *Death in the Afternoon,* he writes:

> I found the greatest difficulty aside from knowing truly what you really felt, rather than what you were supposed to feel, and had been taught to feel; the only thing I could do was to put down what really happened in action.

I have taken examples of literary and communal developments from American literature partly because in some important respects the condition of American literature resembles that of Scottish literature, as does the democratic character of American society. English society is more structured and stratified. Today we recognise its attempts, for instance, to democratise its educational system. Further novelists of quality — until comparatively recently at least — in England have consciously addressed themselves to a stratum. (Consider the cases of Virginia Woolf and Iris Murdoch.) In Scotland even though the sales of novels and poems suggest a limited number of readers, nevertheless the address is to a people. The assumption is not consciously made, but the language of the poet, novelist and dramatist and his material have been evidently given him or her by his people.

The persistence of these assumptions may indicate that Scottish society, despite technological adaptations, has retained something of its integrity, enough perhaps to allow for adaptation, as against disintegration. We can now observe the development of a renewed litery tradition in Scots, English and Gaelic which in the case of Scots goes back more than fifty years. It began with *The Scottish Chapbook* in 1922 which had as its motto, *Precedents, Not Traditions,* in which Hugh MacDiarmid prophesied that the language best suited to the needs of literature in the twenty-first century was Scots. He demonstrated the subtlety, adaptability and resilience of the Scots tongue in his early lyrics and then in his satire, *A Drunk Man Looks at the Thistle*. His prophecy does not look like being fulfilled, but these poems were the first step towards a renewal of contact with a speech, fragmented and eroded as it has become, which related closely to the day to day activities of Scottish people.

The erosion of the speech has continued, yet in 1948 the late Sydney Goodsir Smith published *Under the Eildon Tree*. Ostensibly twenty-four elegies about the loves of the Makar Smith, this poem is amongst other things a comic, satiric, and sometimes affectionate commentary on the sad condition of 'the Western, flickeran bourgeois world', 'the Halie Kremlin', and Smith himself. Its striking success was due to the poet's ability to create an effective idiom out of Pound's *Homage to Sextus Propertius*, references to the Scottish Medieval Makars, and most strongly the Lowland Scots tongue as it came to the poet's ears in the pubs and streets of Edinburgh. This was not Smith's inheritance for he was born in New Zealand, and his University Education was in England, yet he made the language his own. A similar speech, less adulterated, and more traditional was the inheritance of the poet, Alexander Scott, who was born and brought up in Aberdeen. The speech of this area, frequently referred to as The Doric, on account of its eccentricity from other Lowland Scots—or Lallans—has tended to segregate the literature of Aberdeenshire. But Scott modified the idiom without blunting its ironic edge, so that his vigorous, shrewd, sometimes passionate poetry speaks for the wider community of Scottish speech. From the fifties to the seventies the number of poets using Scots as their medium has increased.

Alexander Scott had written short stories in Scots previously and in so doing was carrying on a tradition of which the most notable practitioner was Lewis Grassic Gibbon. In Gibbon's trilogy of novels—*A Scots Quair*, published in the early thirties, he infiltrates the economical, ironic Aberdeenshire Scots idiom into his English narrative, as well as using it dramatically as the speech of his characters. Despite the difficulty of English and Americans following the dialogue, an adaptation of *Sunset Song*, which retains the Scots in large measure, has been successfully broadcast on English and United States television, with considerable success. That success was due to the recognition by audiences that behind the literature was a specific way of life. The time of the novel is set during the first world war and after. That the tale should so come alive, besides being due to the quality of the work and its adaptation, was also due to the sense of reality in the idiom as it was presented by the actors.

Between the time of writing *A Scots Quair* and the present there have been plays of quality by James Bridie, Robert Kemp and Robert Maclellan. These, however, have not connected so immediately with the style of life of working people as did Grassic Gibbon's, or as did George Blake's novel *The Shipbuilders*, nor as recent plays have done by writers still no older than their forties. *Willie Rough*, a play about the men—and their women—who worked in the shipyards of Clydeside, by Bill Bryden was one of the most striking of these. The central character was made out of the memory of the playright's (William Rough Bryden) grandfather. The play achieved its authority on account of Bryden's meticulous concern to reflect on the stage a way of life, which he had learned about from his own people. Several of the actors in the first production knew intimately the speech of Clydeside and its styles of life—the way in which men walked, the manner in which men handled their tools and took their drink, and their common attitudes to women. Consequently, unlike the majority of English actors, who would have had backgrounds that dissociated them from working people, the Scottish actors did not so much act the parts as become them. By the chance of Bill Bryden being Director of the Royal Lyceum Theatre in Edinburgh the play was first performed there. When it went to Glasgow the Citizens' Theatre was packed with people who wanted to see themselves, people who could feel the tools in their hands, who listened to the rich racy, coarse speech in the knowledge that they were overhearing themselves. Only when this happens is total theatre achieved.

One of the principals in *Willie Rough*, Roddy Macmillan—perhaps the most notable character actor living in Scotland—was apprenticed as a beveller in Glasgow when he was a youth. It was appropriate that shortly after *Willie Rough, The Bevellers* by Roddy Macmillan was given its first performance in the Lyceum. Just as Roddy Macmillan had passed on his intimate knowledge of the small gestures—the setting of a cap at an angle, the raising of a hand to say no, the subtle pitches and movement of the voice—which had earned respect for *Willie Rough* of those who knew, so he gave instruction in the craft of bevelling glass to the other actors in his own play. In the explicit and implicit relationships between playrights and their materials—the craftsmen and their crafts—between the actors and the play and their association with the people who made possible the plays there was shown community. John Grierson, who is generally considered the father of the documentary film once described it as 'the creative treatment of actuality'. The remark relates to the plays under discussion, but it does not take account of the dimension which is more and less in these plays, and in all the writings in Scots to which I have referred, whereby communal modes of feeling, humour and suffering, long established in Scottish life, are given expression. These sporadic dramatic and literary successes reveal the failure of the Scots to capitalise throughout their history on a style of life which called for dramatic expression. What is consequential, however, to this argument, is that the arts provide sufficient evidence of continuities of communal characteristics which stretch from the fifteenth century to the present.

Without these characteristics being present in their social material these plays could not have been produced, nor even more significantly could *Docherty*, a novel by William MacIlvanney, first published in 1975, been achieved. In *Docherty* the texture of a mining community is created through the character of Docherty, a miner, his family and their associates. Though the time of the novel is set in the past the picture is presented with such intimacy and authority, that it is difficult not to believe that the author wrote the book in the knowledge of the idiom of the life as part of his life. He has inherited that past, knowing how the bonds of poverty, necessity and danger bound together the family he describes. In this society the scale of moral values was clear and firm. Theft, violence, fornication, were sins which could be coped with within the social framework, but the rejection of the family, and consequently by implication, the community, was not tolerated.

The strength of the communities out of which these dramatists and writers have come, is in the ability of their mores to absorb tensions. These communities have mores and moralities which have absorbed traditional values which are not the property of any single class of society. Though each of the societies have their differences, they make their moral judgements out of a common ethos. The question to be asked is whether these values may survive in the new mass production society. Does not the evidence point to the desire for higher wages as the sole, significant motivating factor in mass societies. This simplification is paralleled by simplified moralities, which suggests there is little prospect of a continuity of a social identity whereby individuality is sustained. One thinks of the tribal identities of the sects in Northern Ireland and of their counterparts as they are given expression in the sectarian followers of the Rangers and Celtic football teams in Glasgow. These divisions have, of course, historical origins but their character seems now to relate to the mindlessness—sought for, and treasured—of the pop fans, and the hippies whose only hope of satisfaction, is to divest themselves of individual identity.

Such mindlessness reflects a condition of decivilization which threatens not simply a Scottish identity but the continuity of a human identity. When Camus drew hope from the idea of community founded on a common awareness of man's ultimate destruction, he wrote for those only capable of such knowledge. The triviality and parochialism of much writing in Scotland from the twenties to the forties was due to the failure of Scottish writers to take account of the significant directions of writers such as Sartre, Joyce, Proust, Rilke and Kafka. Hugh MacDiarmid was aware of this when he wrote in the first number of *The Scottish Chapbook* in August 1922:

> In my opinion, then, for several generations Scottish literature has neither seen nor heard nor understood what was taking place around it. For that reason it remains a dwarf among giants. Scottish writers have been terrified to appear inconstant to established conventions. They have stood still and consequently been left behind in technique and ideation. Meanwhile the Scottish nation has been radically transformed in temperament and tendency; Scottish life has been given a drastic reorientation with the result that Scottish literature today is in no sense representative or adequate.

Here we need concern ourselves less with the acknowledgement of the continuing life of the Scottish nation in its literature and more with its continuing character.

It seems to me that despite the threat to human identity this small nation is now better equipped to conserve and to develop character than it has been previously in this century. There is increasing awareness of a great need for the practical imagination, for the sense of community, for the recognition of performances of merit in whatsoever fields they occur. Despite the radical transformation of life to which MacDiarmid referred more than fifty years ago, the writings to which I have drawn attention witness to continuities of values, now more necessary than ever before. I may not be able to specify characteristics which together add up to a single identity, but the pressures on the Scottish people and their increasing awareness of their distinctive attitudes and sometimes practices, leads me to risk optimistically the conclusion that the nation's true nature and its appropriate contribution over many fields will be increasingly recognised by other nations. There is less risk of a take-over by admass to the small close-knit nation, especially one with a long attachment to the condition of an educated democracy, than to those nations where conurbation-anonymous plays the dominating role in its society. There is, I believe, a great danger in putting a faith in political readjustments, necessary as these may be, but there is evidence in the increasing attention paid by schools and universities in Scotland to the arts in Scotland that there is a quickening of understanding of what must be promoted through the educational channels for the sake of the survival of character.

I have paid inadequate attention to developments in Gaelic literature which, I believe, despite the decreasing numbers of Gaelic speakers, is now contributing refining qualities to the texture of national experience; nor has comment been made on the developments in music in Scotland, notably in the outstanding achievement of Scottish Opera. Music does not so readily reveal the character of the society, which benefits by it. Yet nothing is more indicative of Scotland stretching itself imaginatively as it has never done previously than the quality of Scottish Opera and the character of the achievement. By the training of the Scottish National Opera Chorus and of the Edinburgh Festival Chorus—both dependent on the work of smaller and less ambitious choruses throughout Scotland— an increasing number of amateur singers have participated in a musical endeavour of wide ranging interests. This achievement differs from that of Sir Hugh Robertson's Glasgow Orpheus Choir which while fulfilling the objectives of the conductor exquisitely, failed to venture into music which was not readily pleasing. Scottish Opera, on the other hand, has included both traditional masterpieces and avant-garde works in its repertoire.

It may well be argued that the impact of 'high' culture on the character of a nation is minimal and especially today, when one of the characteristics of the stratified societies of the twentieth century is the inability of the one level to be leavened by the finer art experience of another. The condition of total non-communication which Martin Pawley forecasts in his book *The Private Future* is the ultimate deterioration. It could be argued that there is presumption in denying 'the right of everyone to his own taste', the other aspect of which phrase is—'It is for the masses'. To me both phrases witness to an abdication of responsibility to those less fortunately provided for. I do not suggest that 'high' culture has necessarily a strong impact on any nation but that rather it is, or should be, an aspect of the life of a nation, which has arisen out of the nation. For instance, whatsoever the percentage of the population of Italy who attend opera, it is difficult to believe that the style of Italian Opera does not relate to the dramatic gestures and speech of the Italian people. Equally, if interest in that opera were to be abandoned in favour of, say, the European Song Contest, that abysmal betrayal of song, and of the character of the national traditions of song which it presumes to present, broadcast annually by the BBC, who would deny that such a change in taste betokened a national deterioration of character! The progress is towards the amalgam which is 'musak'. The blunting of discrimination, and response, and this is the condition required of habitual 'listeners' to background music—has its parallel in failures of moral response. The end product is not a person who chooses what he likes but a victim of mass processes. What we are considering is the condition of a patient; be he Scottish, European or American, his condition is critical.

So long as such a condition is seen simply as an economic, social or political ill—though these aspects are implicated in the condition—so long the fundamental diagnosis may not have been made, and for so long appropriate measures cannot be taken. An infra-structure of moral values, without the existence of which society will collapse is being destroyed. The point at which a stream of cars will pass by a woman lying injured on the road is the point at which humane, responsible social behaviour has ceased to exist. This episode happened in the United States in 1976. The reason given by some drivers for their failure to stop was fear of attack, but when students from several universities in the United States simulated similar situations, the behaviour of passers-by was also inhuman. Only when the episode was enacted on a university campus was help readily offered. There, apparently, some kind of community existed.

The dulling of conscience and consciousness is a characteristic of the society where the individual has no sense of playing a meaningful role in it, wherein he may not affect the conditions of living which society provides for him. A factor of some consequence in the destruction of the individual's moral perceptions, and in consequence of his will to act in situations which call for his intervention as a human being, is living in the presence of mass media whose motivation is profit-making or in the requirement to entertain the greatest number irrespective of the quality or character of the material projected. Both these conditions apply in large measure to broadcasting in the United States, while in the press the disproportionate amount of space given to trivial matters, especially to sport, must obscure for the generality issues of real concern. Two aspects of the situation must be remarked here. In the United States the broadcasting of news items is frequently interrupted by commercial 'breaks', some of which show fictional violence. Even a viewer or listener who sets himself to attend to the News may find difficulty in discriminating between fact and fiction. Ultimately one half-listens, half-looks and allows the images and sounds to flow over one. The other aspect is the denial by such productions of space to those masterpieces of art which are the birthright of the nation. These are informed by the tone, or tones, moral, spiritual and aesthetic, which is evidence of a continuing national and individual character. Such works 'feed back' responses more discriminating and, according to their character, of stronger moral fibre than those which were given by society to their authors. I do not suggest that literature and the arts are all that are required. They themselves speak of national character and are a confirmation of its presence or absence. Without the nutrition of these works a people is the more vulnerable to specious, vulgar appeals. I suggest there is a connection between the deprivation of the young of this inheritance, and consequently of a sense of the meaning of life, and social and cultural vandalism. Had there not been such impoverishment I doubt if the exploitation of adolescent emotions by pop groups such as the Rolling Stones and the Bay City Rollers would be so devastatingly successful as they are; successes achieved in conurbations across the map of the western world. The questions remain, how can personal responsibility and personal response develop in the presence of mass irresponsibility, and where may it do so?

Scotland can be regarded as a useful clinical case. There is evidence on the one hand of the onset of the mass condition, and in a virulent form—wanton violence in the cities, the development of marauding gangs who take their foul language to places of entertainment, and with this the acceptance of the same cultural diet as that which is fed throughout the decivilised west. If that were all that can be said then the identity of Scotland is cosmopolitan anonymous. Equally I suggest that even if the Scots were more conscious of their national past, historical and literary, than they are, this would not halt the general tendency. But there is evidence that resistance in the form of mental and character habits, associated with industry as well as with cultural institutions (I refer to the Law, the Church and Scottish Education) and a growing sense of national purpose give rise to a little hope. Just as the conservation of natural resources, perhaps at the last moment, has become a matter of acute concern on a worldwide scale, so we in Scotland begin to know and value what we have been, what we are, and what we might become.

If this little hope is to become a promise, then it seems to me, we must have the conviction that we have the freedom of Scotland. We must have the right to go about it. We do not have this right at present. You cannot rejoice in a land which is still a game reserve. There are other disinheritances. Still to have this awareness is to point to a continuity of resistant character. That resistance has been too long underground. When Hugh MacDiarmid wrote *A Drunk Man Looks at the Thistle,* except for literary comment, it went unnoticed. T.S. Eliot's *The Waste Land*, published four years previously was taken up, admittedly at one level, as the expression of the disintegration of European culture, throughout the English-speaking world. It pointed to the decline and dissolution of the religious and cultural elements which had stayed the decline. But MacDiarmid's poem, radical as it is in its criticism of Scottish society, implied the existence of strong positives which could still be a resource and not a recourse, to be drawn on for new developments.

The risk is that devolution or national independence will lead to an excess of emphasis on the ethnic aspects of culture in Scotland. The greatness of MacDiarmid's poetry is in its emphasis on the necessity of comprehension, and for the sake of humanity. This has not meant that he has lost his national identity, but his poetry is no closed shop. His poetry has put us in line with those geniuses of the Scottish past, be they doctors, scientists, philosophers or mathematicians, which caused others to respect the finer minds of those people of Scotland who, by their art and science, showed their respect for life. Out of the dire necessity of our times, it may be, Scotland will again show that respect for life, so that we shall cease to export the idea of ourselves as a quaint, peasant people. It is by these concerns, far removed from a preoccupation with the narcissistic concept of 'a Scottish identity' that such an identity will nevertheless present itself. The evidence I have adduced suggest the potential is there. Whether that potential is realised is another matter.

3 MINERAL WEALTH

Donald Duff

There is not, as far as I know, agreement as to what constitute 'natural resources'. In an inventory of Scotland's natural resources one could quite reasonably include its scenery, its land, its birds and animals, its waters and their fishes, its minerals and its people. But there is a fundamental difference between most of the items listed and the ones with which a geologist is concerned. Trees, plants, fish, animals are accepted, in general terms, as renewable resources. However, once removed from the ground, coal, oil or other minerals are finished. Recycling might for a time enable recovery of some of the metals, but once coal and oil are burned they have gone forever.

This chapter is concerned primarily with Scotland's non-renewable resources, but before dealing with them it is instructive to look at one of the more important renewable resources to emphasise the fundamental differences. Scotland has a land area of some nineteen million acres of which ten per cent carries tree crops—yet there were far more tree-covered areas in the past, and we are in the process of increasing our present acreage for the immediate future. If it had not been for the far-sightedness of certain land-owners, as far back as the Middle Ages, there would be no trees. The Gaels, the Angles and the Norsemen ruthlessly cut down trees on the flat ground near the sea where they settled to plant crops. They burned trees from the higher ground to provide ash to enrich the soil around their settlements, while at the same time their animals ate the young seedlings trying to re-establish themselves in the deforested areas. As the centuries wore on additional demands were made on trees for building ships, for charcoal in iron-smelting and so on. At the start of the twentieth century only one million acres of land in Scotland were woodland—all privately owned. In 1919 with the establishment of the Forestry Commission the landowners were joined in their efforts to retain and extend an important natural resource which was in danger of disappearing altogether. At present the Forestry Commission has about one million acres of plantation and is planting at the rate of approximately 45,000 acres per year, while private landowners are working on a similar scale. Apart from the importance of producing home-grown timber so that we do not have to rely exclusively on overseas supplies the industry employs in all its aspects, from growing to marketing, about 9,000 to 10,000 people.[1] Fuels and minerals, however, are a very different type of natural resource—they are independent of climate, for example, which of course is critical for the type of forestry or agriculture carried out, or the types of fish that occur in certain areas.

A country's possession of mineral resources is a matter of geographical luck, combined perhaps with a degree of past political astuteness (and occasional inspired guesswork as to what might lie beneath the soil or the sea). But the findings and exploitation of mineral resources demands geological knowledge, technological skill and a suitable economic climate. Scotland is not over-endowed with mineral resources and it is very unlikely, certainly in its landward area, that anything quite as rich as off-shore oil will turn up so fortuitously at a time of economic decline. Nevertheless it still possesses certain other valuable resources which must be utilised in an intelligent manner. Recently when discussing the planning aspects of mineral exploitation in Britain a Government publication[2] defined the significance of mineral resources as follows:

> It is difficult to exaggerate the importance of minerals to our way of life, our industry and our economy: Fertilisers for agriculture—fossil fuels and uranium for heat, light and power—bricks and mortar, plaster and glass for housing—concrete and steel for major structures—raw materials for the chemical industry—metals of all kinds for light and heavy machinery—vast quantities of aggregates for roads and airports— all are mineral products and all are essential in a densely populated country with a highly developed industrial economy.

Scotland is not a densely populated part of the United Kingdom but despite the importance of agriculture, forestry and fishing it relies mainly on a highly developed industrial economy for its survival and consequently the quotation is apt.

While it is arguably a matter of luck whether or not a country possesses rich mineral resources it is not a matter of luck that particular minerals occur where they do. The different minerals are associated with specific rock assemblages and geologists know enough now to be able to predict the occurrence of particular minerals in certain areas, but it is still impossible to forecast the quantities that will be there. We can list what we now have, and say what we might hope to find and where it will be. But without a considerable amount of expensive drilling and excavation we cannot outline the tenor and dimensions of a deposit and make suggestions as to how, whatever is there, can best be utilised. Modern society needs two sorts of materials—those that produce energy such as coal, oil and uranium, and those that can be used after mining, quarrying and processing by means of this energy—metals, chemicals, building materials and so on.

Currently the responsibility for finding out what Scotland has in the way of mineral resources rests with the Institute of Geological Sciences (formerly the Geological Survey)—which is part of the Natural Environment Research Council. Over the past 100 years the 'Survey' has given an extremely good idea of what there is in the way of rocks and minerals and has published most of this information in geological maps and books, etc.[3] One of the biggest problems continues to be ensuring that the building and civil engineering industries and the planners know what information is available and how to use it. A distinguished English geologist recently said that their education system turns out a geologically illiterate population,[4] and I am afraid the same is true of Scottish education,though the proposed introduction of 'O' grade geology to the Scottish schools in 1978 will obviously help.

Coal has been worked systematically for centuries, output having risen from about half-a-million tons per year in 1700 to a peak of 43 million tons in 1914. Since the first world war output has declined, partly because the easily mineable seams have been worked out and partly because of the advent of cheap oil from abroad. In the 1950s the National Coal Board in Britain supplied something like 90 per cent of the UK's total energy demands—by 1971 this proportion had dropped to 43 per cent. The rather late-in-the-day awareness of the danger of relying too heavily on imported oil has, however, dramatically changed our way of thinking about coal. The sixties were a depressing period for the coal industry with cheap oil from the Middle East and natural gas from the North Sea increasingly supplanting coal in its traditional markets of industry, the railways and the coal-gas industry. The Central Electricity Generating Board (the NCB's largest customer) was also considering going over completely to oil and nuclear fired power stations. In Scotland the number of coal mines fell from 102 in 1966, to 41 in 1975, with annual production of deep-mined coal in that period dropping from 15 million tons to 9.75 million tons.

It is little wonder that unease among the miners about the future of their industry was a contributory factor in the 1972 strike. The Coal Industry Act of 1971 demonstrated that Central Government accepted some financial responsibility for the social problems inherent in pit closures but it did not envisage a change in demand for coal. The 1973 Act, however, went further in accepting that even more of the social costs of closures must be met from Government Funds but it also wrote off accumulated deficits of the NCB and reduced the book value of its assets, thus benefiting the industry by reducing depreciation and capital charges. This latter move, coupled with Government grants in connection with production of coal for power stations, for coking coals and for stock piling, meant the NCB, no longer saddled with past debts, could look to the longer-term future. It is now acknowledged that the coal industry cannot be considered *in vacuo* and in fact has an increasingly important role to play in the future of energy supply.

Scotland will never, using present technologies, be able to produce cheap coal. Nevertheless it does possess considerable reserves at depth and the £1 million exploratory drilling programme embarked on during the past year shows the confidence there is in the future of the industry. Most of the coal occurs in rocks of Carboniferous age located mainly in the Midland Valley of Scotland (Figure 1). Most remaining coal can be used only for electricity generation. Scotland does not appear to possess rich reserves of, for example, coals suitable for steel-making, and while the Lurgi gas-plant at Westfield in Fife is an encouraging feature in that it uses inferior coal from an enormous 'quarry' to produce gas, natural gas from the North Sea gas-fields will probably continue to be the most economic gas for the next few decades. Future developments in the deep-mining of coals in Scotland will therefore be confined to specific areas—areas where there is a guaranteed demand and where the enormous capital investment required to sink new deep mines can be seen to be justified. At the moment it seems most of the newer developments will take place in the Firth of Forth area.

On the southern side the Midlothian Coalfield has been kept in existence by the fact that Cockenzie Power Station was built as a coal-fired station, specifically to use the Midlothian coal. Drilling operations offshore in 'the Forth have proved the continuation of the coalfield under the sea-bed and there are proved reserves of 50 million tonnes of coal. The Fife coalfield also extends seawards though steeply dipping seams will make mining difficult. There are still possibilities in the central portion of the Forth between the extensions of the two coalfields and probably off other parts of Fife too but for the immediate future the upper Forth estuary in the Longannet-Clackmannan area is being drilled, with promising results. In central Scotland, in the Fauldhouse area, indications are that coal suitable for blending for coke-manufacture is available in promising amount, while further west the Ayrshire Coalfield has ample reserves suitable for power-station and domestic use. The problem here at the moment is that of suitable markets as indeed is the case if development of reserves available in the Douglas and Canonbie Coalfields is contemplated. Moving further into the realms of speculation there is every

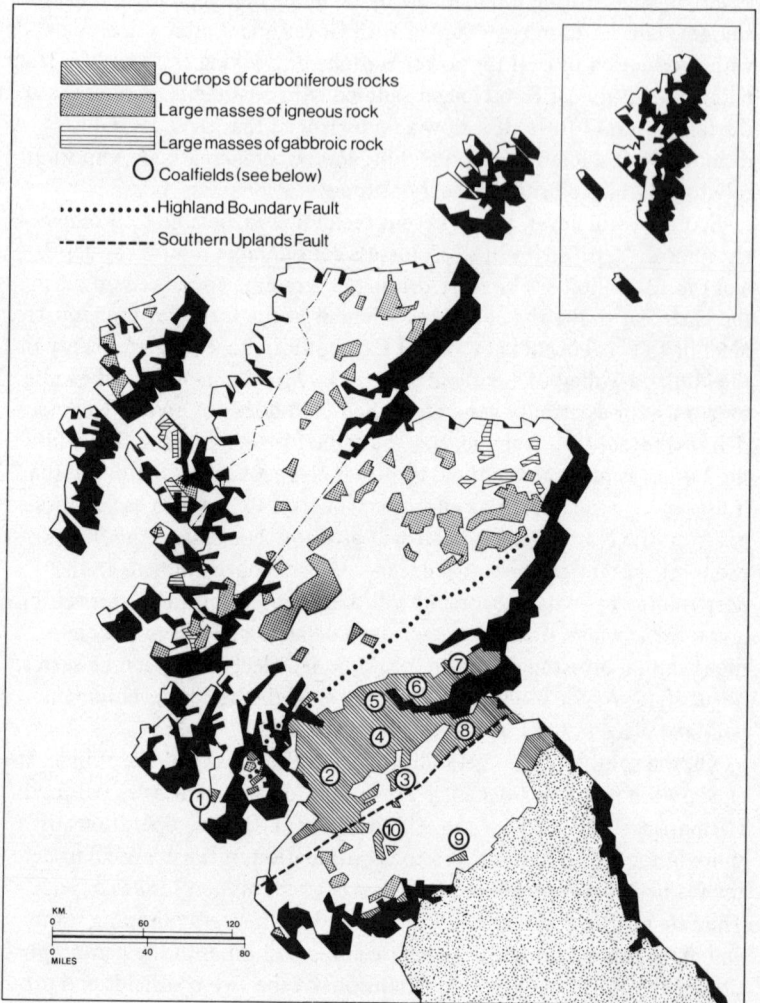

Figure 1. This map shows Scotland's three structural regions which are created by the two major faults. The Southern Uplands are mainly older sedimentary rocks, and igneous rocks. The Midland Valley contains mainly Carboniferous and Permian sedimentary and igneous rocks. The structure north of the Highland Boundary Fault is mainly of older metamorphic rocks and igneous rocks of varying ages. Within this northern region there are two other prominent faults; the Moine Thrust Fault which runs south from Durness through Loch Kishorn, and the Great Glen Fault between Inverness and Loch Linnhe. The coalfields marked on the map are: 1 Machrihanish 2 Ayrshire 3 Douglas 4 Central 5 Stirling 6 Clackmannan 7 Fife 8 Lothians 9 Canonbie 10 Sanquhar.

reason to be optimistic about the possibility of Jurassic coal below the Moray Firth as a logical corollary to its occurrence at Brora—though admittedly it is not of high quality there.

The future for coal is therefore hopeful as far as workable reserves are concerned but mining conditions will on the whole be challenging. The relative thinness of the seams, their depth below the ground and a variety of geological problems render the problems among the greatest I have ever seen in coalfields throughout the world. In Scotland the output per man shift is about two tons, whereas in the USA output per man shift is 32-36 tons from open-pits and from their so-called deep mines all shallower by a factor of two or three compared with Scottish deep mines, output per man shift is about ten tons. These figures should not be taken as a criticism of Scottish miners or mining methods. The figures reflect the difficult mining conditions.

Opencast mining is still a practical proposition in many parts of the coalfield areas, with Westfield in Fife being an example of one of the largest operations in Britain. Environmental considerations are paramount with this type of mining and it should be said that the NCB is among the world leaders in proper restoration of sites. They have recognised that there is no excuse for the unbelievable ravages of the land carried out in the past and have shown all over Britain what can be done in the way of restoration. During mining operations there is no way an opencast site can look like anything but a severe blot on the landscape but afterwards there is every possibility that no trace will be left and that on occasions the land may be improved agriculturally or scenically. The amount of opencast mining to be carried out in Scotland, apart from pure geological aspects, can only be determined by careful consideration of economic, social and environmental problems at the time of the proposed mining operations. Its practice will not permanently ruin the land as well-meaning, but sometimes ill-informed, conservationists claim. Currently Scotland produces about 1.8 million tons annually by opencast methods (1.3 million tons at Westfield) and it could be more.

The point must be made, however, before leaving the subject of coal that all the foregoing figures and assumptions are based on current mining practice. Because of the geological complexities, I do not see a situation where mining can be done by remote control and that thin seams, at present unworkable, will be worked by machines and computers. Nevertheless the fact remains that much more coal is left in the ground than is ever mined. If an economic and efficient method to convert coal seams into gas underground,[5] without the need for mining, can be devised, then the reserves of coal available for converting into energy, in

Scotland alone, would probably increase by a factor of ten. There is also the possibility of the controlled burning of coal underground producing heat which could be utilised for various projects.

Oil has been known to exist in Scotland for hundreds of years; in fact the alleged medicinal properties of some ancient wells in Edinburgh owe their peculiar nature to contamination by oil from underground. But unlike coal, oil has not previously been produced for use in Scotland as a fuel in its natural form. Oil shale, however, did play an important part in Scotland's industrial history. Oil shale does not contain oil, it contains organic material which on heating at high temperatures gives off alkanes and other hydrocarbons similar to those in naturally-occurring petroleums. Oil shales are similar to ordinary shales in that they are consolidated clays and muds, but they were deposited in water where there was an abundance of organic material such as algae, plankton, and spores which formed an organic ooze. Shales formed in this way are only preserved occasionally in the geological record. In Scotland they occur in several seams of Lower Carboniferous age in West Lothian.

The industry started in Bathgate in 1851 with a special type of coal as the original raw material but in 1858 oil shale was discovered in the vicinity and it continued to be worked until the industry closed down in 1962. The removal of an excise duty preference combined with the ever-increasing costs of underground mining, and the subsequent processing of the shale at the surface in order to yield perhaps twenty gallons of oil from each ton, meant shale oil could no longer compete with imported oil. There are probably 75 million tons of oil shale which would yield perhaps 14 gallons of oil per ton, still available underground in West Lothian.[6] But present mining and processing methods would barely make the oil end-product competitive. Again methods of *in situ* conversion of the shale to oil underground might yet make a revival of the industry possible, though attempts in 1958 to achieve such a conversion proved unsuccessful.

Because of seepages into coal mines in the Lothians and in other areas of Carboniferous rocks in the Midland Valley the presence of oil was known. Exploratory drilling took place in the period 1919-22, in 1937, in 1944-5, in 1954, 1963 and in the late sixties in various areas of the Lothians and Fife for both oil and natural gas, which frequently occur together. Enough gas was found at Cousland to enable Musselburgh's supply of coal-gas to be augmented from 1957 onwards. Methane gas from coal-mines in Fife and Lanarkshire has also been utilised locally. The possibility of future on-shore oil and gas discovery in Scotland is not promising, however. Suitable rocks are restricted mainly to the Midland

Valley and the most obvious places have already been drilled. The position off-shore is of course a different matter. The discovery of an enormous reservoir of natural gas in rocks of Permian age near Groningen, Holland in 1959 and the knowledge that gas had been recorded in the 1940s in rocks of similar age in Yorkshire awakened the interest of the oil companies in what lay beneath the North Sea. Before then no gas or oil in quantity had been discovered in the rocks surrounding the North Sea and this along with the fact that there was no international agreement as to how the North Sea would be divided up had naturally tended to discourage interest.

By the end of the nineteenth century it had more or less been accepted that a country's claims to the sea and sea-bed off its shores extended to a distance of three nautical miles. Not all countries had agreed, however, and the twentieth century saw the continuation of a series of fundamental disagreements. The 1958 Geneva Convention (and subsequent *Annexes*) on the Territorial Sea and Contiguous Zone went a long way in setting up agreed guidelines for defining a country's sovereign rights to the sea and sea-bed off its shores. It was not until 1964, however, that Britain finally accepted the principles for dividing up the North Sea. Basically the suggestion was that where several countries faced on to such a continental shelf area (defined for the purposes of the 1958 Convention as seabed under less than 200 metres of water) a median line would be drawn equidistant from the opposing shores. Britain was thus given rights to the western half of the North Sea bed, the eastern half being divided between six other countries. There was, and still is, room for dispute, notably over the problems of deciding, what is continental shelf; where is the base-line from which a country's rights extend seawards, for example, should it start from the mainland or from off-shore islands; and how should an international border be continued seawards from the point it reaches the accepted base-line? Currently Britain has not yet reached agreement with France, Ireland or Norway over the division of the seas. The complications that would result if Scotland became independent need not be stressed, and were Orkney and Shetland to have some separate arrangement, the situation would be even more complex. Under the present 'rules' Scotland could lose all rights to the richest oilfields so far discovered in the North Sea.

It is possible by use of geophysical methods to outline areas at considerable depths below the surface and beneath the seabed, where rocks capable of holding oil or gas occur. It should be realised, however, that while oil and gas occur in the pores of rocks such as limestones and sandstones (reservoir rocks), for a variety of reasons not all limestones and sandstones in fact contain them. Even when oil and gas do occur they may not be in sufficient quantity to justify the cost of extraction, nor is it always possible to get them out because of low permeability in the reservoir rocks. Having outlined *possible* oil-bearing areas therefore the next step is to drill into the rocks of those areas—an incredibly difficult, expensive and often dangerous operation at sea. Results in the shallow southern part of the North Sea in 1965 yielded quantities of gas beyond all expectations, and combined with later discoveries this has led to conversion of appliances throughout Britain to natural gas. Little or no oil was discovered and it was not until 1970 that the first commercial discovery of oil was made in UK waters, the Forties Field.

Interestingly enough the oil in the northern part of the North Sea and the gas in the southern sector have completely different geological origins. The gas beneath the southern area is thought to be caused by the heating up of Carboniferous coals below the Permian reservoir rocks. The northern sector gas, however, is believed to have an origin in common with the oil, though its exploitation may be difficult because so much of it occurs in very small pockets. Since 1970 further UK discoveries have been made in the northern part of the North Sea, notably off the Shetlands, and attention is now being directed to waters off the west coast of Scotland, where geophysical surveys have indicated considerable areas of potential reservoir rocks.

The euphoria associated with the discovery of oil around Scotland's coast should however be tempered by looking at the published facts concerning reserves.[7] Published figures of *proven* oil reserves in Britain's continental shelf area give a figure of 1,350 million tonnes, though this is a very conservative figure. A more likely ultimate figure is thought to be in the 3,000-4,500 million tonnes range. World 'proven' reserves are currently calculated at 90 billion tonnes.[8] Even taking our most optimistic estimate Britain's oil accounts for only five per cent of the world's resources, and is more generally accepted as being nearer two per cent. To regard Britain's off-shore oil as another Middle East, which has half the world's 'proven' reserves, is nonsense. Against an exponential rise in world consumption, now about 3 billion tonnes per year, it can be seen that oil may cease to be available quite early in the twenty-first century. It seems completely unrealistic to expect that Scotland will have exclusive rights to supplies of oil for any longer than the rest of the world, particularly as she is short of most other minerals and must rely on international trade and goodwill for their supply. Alternatives to oil will have to be found. In the meantime such financial benefits that will accrue should be seen solely as a temporary relief to a chronic balance of payments problem. What must be ensured now is that capital is immediately available to develop new coal mines that can exploit the fuel there is and to fund research into methods of producing other forms of energy including solar, tidal and geothermal.

In 1962 a survey[9] indicated that about 1,700,000 acres of Scotland is covered by peat to a depth of 2ft or more. In terms of workable peat deposits something like 600 million tons of peat solids are available. On a strictly commercial basis it seemed in 1962 that peat was unlikely to be able to compete with oil or coal as a fuel. Perhaps, however, it would be profitable to study more carefully the methods of harvesting and utilising peat developed by the Irish Bord na Mona (Peat Board). Not only is their peat competing with imported fuels and a variety of by-products being produced but they have shown how rural communities can be revitalised, and Scotland's biggest peat deposits are in areas infamous for depopulation.

Uranium is the remaining fuel to discuss but it is perhaps best considered along with what are called ore minerals (which are economic deposits of metals) as it occurs along with them rather than with the other fuels. Scotland has a long history of producing such metals as iron, lead, zinc, copper, and silver. The iron ore which was once mined occurred with the coal seams and when, at the end of the eighteenth century, coal rather than charcoal was the obvious choice for smelting iron ore so the iron industry developed in the coal areas. The iron ores are in thin beds and low in iron content, so cheaper and richer imported ores soon supplanted the Scottish ores completely during this century. It is almost inconceivable that Scotland should ever exploit its own ironstones again, since there is no shortage of rich iron ore in the world.

The occurrence of other metals is very different and one cannot be so definite as to potential future finds and uses. So far not very much has been found though there is a wealth of information available of what has been worked and discovered to date. The correct types of rocks exist but they apparently do not have enriched portions carrying the metals one might reasonably expect to find. Granites for example, are the rocks which often carry tin, yet Scotland's are barren. Similarly the rock gabbro and kindred rock types in other parts of the world often carry nickel or chromium or platinum in economic quantities, but Scotland's deposits which occur in the Cuillins, in Rhum, in Ardnamurchan and in parts of Aberdeenshire have so far proved disappointing. There are, however, some encouraging tangible signs of potentially useful copper deposits in the Western Highlands and in Shetland. More speculatively, possibilities of new lead and zinc deposits are being investigated.

The whole question of the occurrence of metalliferous deposits is scientifically a very complicated one. The most important point is to ensure that funds are available for both Government bodies and Universities to study further Scotland's mineral potential, principally by mapping, exploration, drilling and laboratory studies, and the mining companies should be encouraged to prospect. It is important to differentiate between exploration where the environmental problems are negligible, and exploitation which requires environmental and social problems to be comprehensively examined. Knowledge of Scotland's potential resources could prevent panic exploitation or expensive buying from overseas, and allow a proper evaluation of her position in the world context of mineral supplies. The growth of the world's population and industrialisation has caused the consumption of more minerals in the last 50 years than in the whole of previous history. Obviously the future of the world's mineral resources is an international problem and Scotland, like all small countries, will survive as an industrial nation only whilst international trade and goodwill allows.

There are of course other metallic minerals in Scotland apart from those mentioned which require further investigation but perhaps most important at the moment is uranium. Potentially workable deposits exist, and notably in Caithness and in Orkney. Currently the deposits are uneconomic but again the world situation cannot be ignored because they are strategic minerals as well as potential fuel minerals. A recent summary of the world position[10] indicates that requirements will far exceed known reserves after 1990 if steps are not taken now to prospect for new sources, and to develop breeder reactors. There are obviously grave problems associated with nuclear power but it would be short-sighted not to continue to look for and assess uranium deposits.

Industry does not of course rely simply on metals. In fact such everyday materials as aggregate for cement and roadstone are second in value only to coal in Scotland in mineral production. There are abundant supplies of such materials, transport costs being probably the biggest economic problem. Limestone, for cement manufacture and for agricultural purposes, is not in quite such abundance but then there is always the possibility of exploitation of off-shore shell sands in the future. Scotland could easily be self-sufficient in building stones but yet stones comparable to those available in Scotland are imported.

Water is a commodity Scotland has in abundance. Surface supplies alone are more than adequate for the forseeable future. Underground sources are barely tapped and their potential scarcely studied. Surely the time has come to study properly Scotland's water resources, to up-grade the distribution system within Scotland and to consider seriously the possibility of exporting some by pipe-line to England.

To sum up then, Scotland is not over-endowed with mineral wealth but there is plenty of evidence indicating that we are not making full use of what we have.

Notes

1. Forestry Commission. *Forestry in Scotland.* HMSO, Edinburgh, 1973.

2. Department of the Environment etc. *Planning Control over Mineral Working.* HMSO, London, 1976.

3. Bulletins, Memoirs, Reports and Special Reports of the Geological Survey of Scotland and Great Britain and the Institute of Geological Sciences, HMSO. (For complete list of publications see *Government Publications Sectional List No. 45,* HMSO, London; for a list of geological maps see *Map Catalogue,* Ordnance Survey (T. Nelson & Sons, 18 Dalkeith Road, Edinburgh).)

4. Royal Society of London. 'A discussion on the exploitation of British mineral resources (other than coal and hydrocarbons) in relation to countryside conservation.' *Proc. Roy. Soc. Lond. (A) 339, 271-416,* 1974.

5. National Coal Board. *Underground gasification of coal—a National Coal Board reappraisal.* NCB, London, 1976.

6. Department of Energy. 'United Kingdom oil shales. Past and future exploitation.' *Energy Paper No. 1.* HMSO, London, 1975.

7. Department of Energy. *Development of the oil and gas resources of the United Kingdom.* HMSO, London, 1976.

8. Institute of Petroleum. *Know more about oil.* World Statistics, Inst. Pet. London, 1976.

9. Department of Agriculture and Fisheries for Scotland. *Scottish Peat.* 2nd Rept. Scott. Peat Committee, HMSO, Edinburgh, 1962.

10. Bowie, S.H.U. 'Whither uranium?' *Trans. Instn. Min. Metall.* 85, B163-9, 1976.

General References

Mineral Resources Consultative Committee *Mineral Dossiers.* HMSO, London.

Duff, P. McL. D. 'Economic Geology' in Craig, G.Y. (ed.) *Geology of Scotland,* Oliver & Boyd, Edinburgh, 1965.

Gallagher, M.J. *et al.* 'New evidence of uranium and other mineralization in Scotland.' *Trans. Instn. Min. Metall. 77,* B150-73, 1971.

George, T.N. 'Economic Minerals in Scotland' in *Natural Resources in Scotland,* 28-56, Scottish Council (Development and Industry), Edinburgh, 1961.

Acknowledgments

I am grateful to the assistance given to me by Mr G. Gillespie and Dr R. Beveridge of the NCB, Mr A.A. Archer of the Institute of Geological Sciences and the Information Service of the Institute of Petroleum. It must be emphasised, however, that the opinions expressed in this chapter and any errors of fact are the sole responsibility of the author.

4 THE GROWTH OF THE ENERGY INDUSTRIES

John Francis

The growth of the energy industries in Scotland is now widely appreciated as an accumulating series of events of national significance. The period from 1970 to 1982 will almost entirely come to be regarded as the transition phase from a position of balanced scarcity of supply to one of relative abundance as far as the domestic markets are concerned. This short review is an attempt to set down the position at the end of 1974, with a backward glance at the reference point in 1970 and with an appreciation of the potential expansion of nearly all forms of energy production in Scotland up to and including Britain's year of 'self-sufficiency' in 1982. It can hardly be disputed that this is the period that will change the face of the national fuel economy almost beyond recognition. Within Scotland, in particular, it will bear testimony to the struggle to stabilise and possibly to optimise output in the coalfields; it will launch the new offshore oil and gas industry into its most expansive phase and it will also witness the consolidation of nuclear power as the baseline for the electricity supply network. It is the purpose of this review to draw some of the disparate threads of this argument together, to integrate them in a straightforward manner and in the process, to reveal some of the essential weaknesses in the competition that takes place between the fuel industries.

The advent of North Sea Oil and Gas is an explosion of energy availability, compared with the almost leisurely changes in the 1946 to 1970 period resulting from the decline of coal production from 24.0 million tons in 1951 to 12.5 million tons in 1970. The shortfall in coal supplies and the increased demand for energy were in this case easily matched by the import of relatively cheap fuel oils even although an exchequer surcharge of £2 per ton was applied and periodically increased. Electricity generation also advanced during this period through the introduction of major hydroelectric schemes and some gas turbines to supplement and to diversify steam generation sources. Diesel generation for the islands, subsidised to some extent by the cheaper hydroelectric power, has given reliable service and is probably destined for further development. The production of manufactured gas had reached its peak by 1970 with the industry having systematically explored the potential of various alternative processes (including coal to gas and crude petroleum to gas conversions); the immediate supply prospects for the period under study appear to be geared exclusively to the production of natural gas from North Sea reserves.

Today, the primary fuels—Coal, Oil and Natural Gas—are in reasonably abundant supply in Scotland, at a price. An examination of the accompanying individual fuel reviews and graphs will show this in more detail. While it is still difficult to appreciate the magnitude of proven North Sea Oil and Gas finds it is important to realise the change of perspective that will be necessary within the Scottish fuel economy. Fuel pipelines are being constructed to bring oil from the Forties field to Cruden Bay and Frigg field natural gas to St. Fergus near Peterhead. These two lines alone will supply more oil and gas than Scotland will need from 1977 onwards; the high pressure pipelines from the Frigg system will obviously be a major artery for the national gas grid that is nearing completion. The crude oil that is surplus to refinery requirements at Grangemouth will be exported via a terminal on the Firth of Forth at Dalmeny. In addition, of course, there are the other massive proven reserves on the UK Continental Shelf which will be piped to Shetland and to Orkney or loaded on tankers at single-point mooring systems for transportation to other UK and European refineries. For the purpose of this survey, it is necessary to identify the potential supplies of solid, liquid and gaseous fuels available to Scottish industry at prices yet to be decided. The impact of new refineries with their associated product spectrum should also be considered in the context of the Scottish fuel economy.

From now on it appears that each sector of the Scottish fuel market will be under increasing competitive pressure from coal, oil, gas and electricity distributors as probable price parities and future supply patterns are established. At present, a rough allocation of the market among the various fuels takes place as follows:

Coal: 60 per cent to power stations, 25 per cent to boiler plants, 15 per cent to coke ovens and to other users.

Gas: Domestic/commercial usage increasing, but volume of industrial requirement doubling every three years and becoming a major industrial fuel outlet by 1975.

Oil: Inter-company competition for aviation fuels, motor spirit, derv, gas oils, petroleum gases, petro-chemical feedstock, lubricating oils and bitumen. General competition from natural gas and coal for power stations, furnaces, boiler plants, brick kilns, distilleries etc. North Sea Oil is of high quality 35^0-44^0 API, 0.2 per cent to 0.4 per cent by weight of sulphur (unlike the high sulphur content of most imported crude oils which lead to environmental and low temperature corrosion problems). Indeed it may still be necessary to import some heavy fuel oils where a high luminosity is required in open hearth furnaces, soaking pits etc.

Electricity: Mainly traditional markets with increased supplies to new industries and steel production more than off-setting stagnation in heating loads.

This section will attempt to describe movements in the primary fuel market (solid fuels, petroleum fuels, natural gas, nuclear and hydro-electricity) during the period under review. Violent fluctuations in demand are usually short lived; discontinuities of supply due to weather, industrial action or major breakdowns have been discounted in this exercise. Generally speaking, the development of demand must be preceded by the installation of distributor's facilities as temporary supply arrangements for significant users are uneconomical. It will become more fashionable in industry to become 'dual fuel' users with oil/gas burners even although such unpopular facilities from the oil companies' view, attract certain price penalty clauses in their supply contracts. Oil and gas are expensive to store in significant quantities and are at their best price in continuous supply conditions varied only by seasonal weather fluctuations.

Solid Fuels

The National Coal Board acknowledge that although a new energy situation exists throughout Britain the contribution of the coal industry will be dependent on several factors:

(a) the growth in UK energy requirements;
(b) the availability of natural gas;
(c) the price relationship between coal and oil;
(d) the power station building programme, particularly the rate at which nuclear power is expanded.

While these complex variables undoubtedly govern the future supply prospects for coal, it is already apparent that any overall strategy leading to stabilisation of the industry must also embrace substantial additional output to offset losses through exhaustion. The declining output from Scottish coalfields during the 1960s (Figure 1) has mirrored the rapid

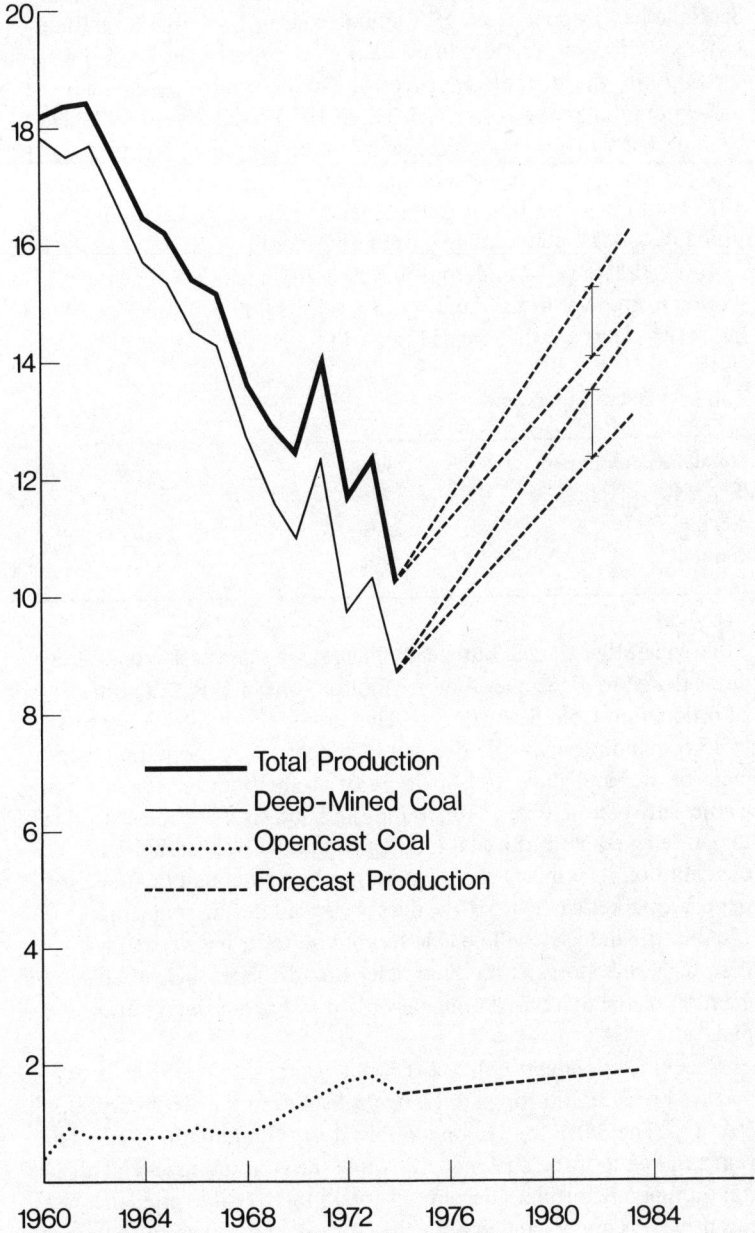

Figure 1. Coal production.

rundown of the industry throughout the rest of the country. Output in Scotland has dropped from 18.2 million tons in 1960 to 12.5 million tons in 1970, and decreases in production are almost certain to be carried forward into the current year's figures. On the credit side the decrease in underground manpower from 24,200 in 1970 to 22,300 in 1973 has been partially offset by an increase in production from 365 tons to 419 tons per man-year. This pattern might be expected to continue until 1980 with modernisation investment and better pay and conditions probably at least maintaining output at present levels.

It is estimated that under favourable economic conditions the underground manpower in Scotland could reach 28,000 in 1982. The following assumptions are then made (Table 1).

Table 1: Deep-mined coal

Production output per man-year	Power Loading	Gross output
450 tons	88%	12.60 million tons
495 tons	98%	13.86 million tons

Provided that a small but steady increase in open-cast production can be sustained to reach a level of 1.8 million tons in 1982, then the potential production from Scottish coalfields should lie within the range 14.4 to 15.6 million tons. While this would appear to represent a massive increase over and above today's levels of production, in actual fact this would only restore output to around the 1966 figure. Subject to this target being realised, the coal industry can effectively stabilise its contribution to primary energy consumption in Scotland with a 30 per cent market share at 1974 prices. It is a matter of conjecture whether the industry will be able to hold on to its market share if their biggest customers, the Electricity Boards, show their disenchantment with coal by constructing new plant to use anything but solid fuel.

Recent Government policy has effectively given the coal industry massive protection through operating subsidies to the electricity supply industry. The SSEB for example received £1.93 million in 1973 to prevent run down of the coal industry while the continuing levy of £1 per ton on fuel oil continues despite this fuel's unavoidable price increase recently. It is understandable for the Government to keep this truly indigenous fuel supply viable. Both the NCB and the trade unions can obviously draw their own inferences from the Power Boards decision. With transport costs looming high in the final price structure of coal, the industry must be examined in terms of its future competitive position in the Scottish fuel market. Since the revival of expectations in some English coalfields, particularly North Yorkshire and the new Selby promise, these may conceivably challenge the already marginal position of the output from some Scottish fields.

The November 1974 Budget statement has clearly indicated that a full competitive position should be restored within the nationalised fuel industries as soon as possible. In terms of the above argument, this could have quite serious implications for the future of the coal industry in Scotland. From Figure 1, it is evident that a major reorientation of the industry will be necessary if the decline is to be arrested. A failure to retain the present share of existing markets could lead to a total production of only eight to ten million tons per annum in the early 1980s. In the present market, SSEB have already demonstrated their ability to burn at least eight million tons per annum, and this is the factor which largely determines the lower-end of the range. Although it is now recognised that there will be a surplus of electrical generating capacity in Scotland by 1980, there is some speculation within the coal industry leading to the view that if Scottish coal was to become cheaper than imported fuel oil, coal-fired stations could displace some of the oil-fired capacity.

The NCB estimate that the demand for coal at a national level will be in the range 120 to 150 million tons by 1985 (the 1973 to 1974 demand figures are already close to the median point of the range, i.e. 133 million tons). The suggested pattern of investment at a total capital cost of £600 million (in addition to the £70 to £80 million per annum required for ordinary continuing capital expenditure) would be designed to yield over 40 million tons of new capacity by the mid-1980s, but does not apparently include any major expansion of Scottish capacity. In the period up to 1982, the Scottish coal industry has a major requirement to stabilise the output of deep-mined coal, and to improve performances through increased mechanisation and productivity agreements. It is assumed that the industry will receive sufficient encouragement from the Government of the day to maintain a 30 per cent share of the primary energy market in Scotland i.e. the industry will be required to conduct a holding operation but at production levels well above the 1974 average. Future confidence and investment prospects for this industry in Scotland will undoubtedly be governed by the ability of the industry to achieve this target.

Petroleum Fuels

After two decades of competition with coal, the Scottish fuel oil market-
ers had successfully penetrated into steel plants, electricity and general
industry by 1970 with their relatively cheap and easy-to-handle liquid
fuels. Road, rail and coastal tanker deliveries were also well established by
this time. The 'dual-fuel' users such as Electricity Boards were assisted
in overcoming the successive periods of crisis and industrial unrest in the
coalfields. The recent increases of price by the OPEC countries have in
turn generated threefold increases in the supply price to power stations
in as many months. This effect is masked in the energy statistics by the
1974 miners' strike otherwise the downturn in fuel oil deliveries would
have been much greater. As it was, the SSEB took 285,000 tons less during 1973 to 1974 than in the previous year. With almost daily increases
in competition from natural gas in the fuel oil and liquefied petroleum
gas market, the outlook to 1980 for liquid petroleum fuels looks bleak.
This is recognised by the oil companies, although the effect on reduced
employment will be confined to only a small number of drivers and
technical sales staff. By its international nature the oil companies can
sell the oil in other energy-hungry countries at a high price. The only
major refinery in Scotland at Grangemouth, which produces fuel oil
during the process of extracting the lighter petroleum fractions, will not
be significantly affected by these price movements.

The trend in inland petroleum consumption via the Scottish market
is outlined in Figure 2. This graph effectively integrates the various fuel
oil grades supplied to industry, and also includes the quantities of kero-
sene and gas oils used for central heating purposes. There seems very
little doubt that new central heating business has been more or less con-
ceded to natural gas-firing, although existing consumers are fairly slow
to respond to price fluctuations thus stabilising the current pattern of
demand. This time-lagged element in the demand curve applies equally
to large consumers such as the steel industry and the Electricity Board,
which should allow some re-structuring of the primary fuel market to
take place. Under current economic constraints, the movement is very
much away from an increasing dependency on the petroleum fuel section.
There are, however, a number of reasons why the consumption is buffer-
ed against the major price increases that have already been registered.

Until power stations started to use oil in significant quantities in the
1960s, steel plants with their open hearth furnaces, blast furnaces and
soaking pits were the largest users of fuel oil. Electric and other methods
of converting iron into steel will now gradually replace the tilting and
fixed open hearth furnaces, with gas taking over from oil in soaking pits.

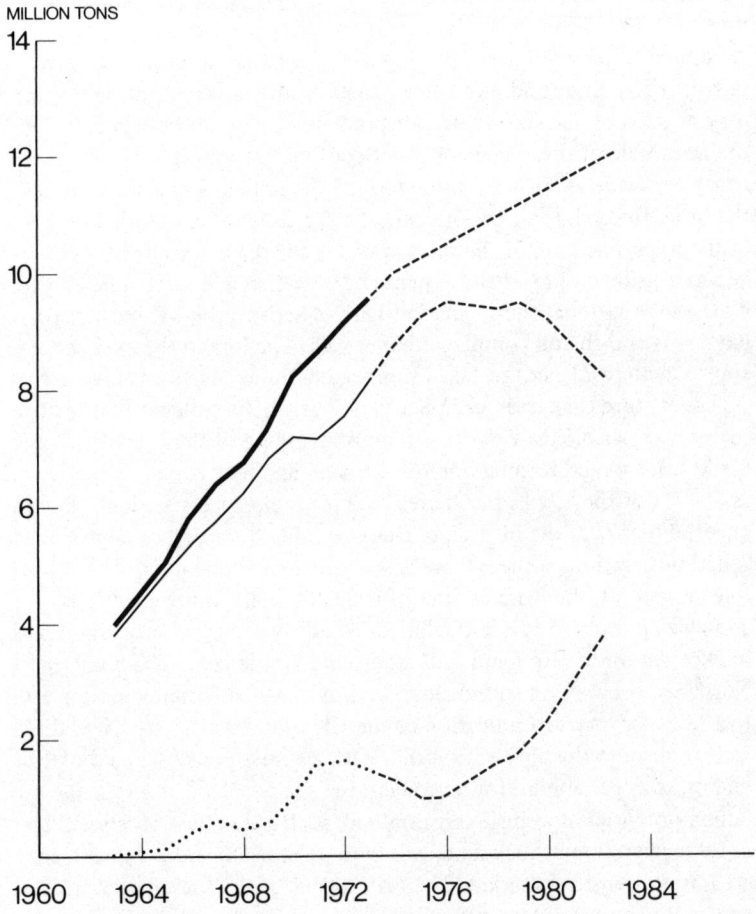

Figure 2. Inland petroleum fuels consumption.

Fortunately for the oil companies Inverkip and Carolina Port power
stations are designed solely for fuel oil—at the moment. Had there been
no OPEC price convulsion in 1973 to 1974, these stations when fully
commissioned by 1977 would have been using approximately 3.2 million
tons per annum. When added to the requirements for Peterhead oil-fired
station, due to produce power in 1978, the figures for fuel oil consumption in 1974 are almost doubled; this trend is also evident in Figure 2.
A number of new refineries are proposed for Scotland using imported
or North Sea crude and exporting products; the resultant refinery gases
may be used by the Gas Board but production will not be significant in
the time-scale of this review. A number of oil/gas strikes in the northern
North Sea were announced throughout 1974, which when added to all
the other finds and sources of energy, will necessitate a detailed review
of the price structure of the fuels available for the country's industry.
Gas expansion will be at the expense of oil which will in turn be absorbed
by the international energy market with benefit to the UK balance of
payments and the oil companies concerned. The loss to the exchequer of
approximately £1 per ton tax is submerged in the large sums involved.

The picture that emerges in Scotland over the petroleum fuel sector is
the perhaps surprising view of a diminishing share of the primary energy
market. A marked turning point in demand has been already experienced
as a result of the 1974 price increases. Future prospects are hedged with
uncertainties over the future policies governing the firing of large electrical
generating stations. Unless there is some further trauma in the world petroleum market, the massive sales of heavy fuel oils to the electricity
industry appear to provide the buffer conditions necessary to stabilise the
market share for petroleum fuels at around 40 per cent. The build-up of
North Sea production to the alleged point of self-sufficiency during 1981
to 1982 is of course a reflection of the UK demand estimates. It is difficult to dispute the observation that with an anticipated demand of 12
million tons per annum for petroleum fuels in Scotland in 1982, the production potential of a single large oilfield, such as Forties, which will be
in full production at that time, will more than balance the demand generated by the Scottish market. The disturbance of the fuel market in Scotland is, of course, potentially much greater through some radical changes
in the fuel mix involving widespread distrubution of natural gas to domestic and industrial consumers. These substitution effects will almost certainly emerge as the most crucial aspect of the Scottish energy situation
during the next ten year investment period. The new era of energy conservation and optimisation of end-use will substantially condition the
strategies for the use of petroleum fuels, probably more than any other

comparable raw material, but no major changes in the pattern of use can be anticipated before 1980 at the very earliest.

Natural Gas Supplies

The Scottish Gas Board, which became the Scottish Region of British Gas on 1 January 1974, is preparing to meet the largest market demand together with a corresponding flow of abundant supplies that the area has ever known. Production methods have previously been based on coal and naptha, but town gas, carburetted water gas, lurgi and coke oven gas are now all being rapidly replaced by natural gas from offshore reserves. The new replacement fuel is even considered as a serious economic possibility for central power station use and also for boiler plants throughout Scotland, although both of these applications are far from the premium market that has been secured for natural gas. The premium market exists because of the special advantages that are linked with the utilisation of natural gas, viz., that it is a clean fuel and susceptible to a fine degree of control in most heating applications. It remains to be seen whether natural gas can find a place in the bulk industrial and commercial markets that is compatible with an optimum allocation policy by price.

An indication of the output that British Gas is arranging to supply in the period up to 1982 is shown in Figure 3. The anticipated expansion of demand in the post-1972 period is already substantially under way, and clearly suggests that natural gas will have a significant future role in shaping the Scottish fuel economy. High pressure gas mains have been installed throughout the central industrial belt and currently extend as far north as Dundee. The investment programme is geared to the quantities indicated in Figure 3 with increased penetration of the existing fuel oil markets and through rising central heating sales. The use of natural gas as a potential fuel for power stations is not included in these forward estimates. It has been argued elsewhere that growth of the premium markets will not be anything like sufficient to absorb the available gas as supplies build up from the North Sea. While depletion policies for individual North Sea fields will be governed by investment in transmission and distribution facilities, there will undoubtedly be further Government statements on the optimisation of the market for natural gas. The competitive pricing of natural gas on an equivalent heat content basis will serve to redress the balance (see later section on pricing).

The British Gas Corporation, which registered a loss of £41.3 million in the financial year 1975-6, has already implemented an average increase of twenty per cent on industrial and business tariffs; it is anticipated

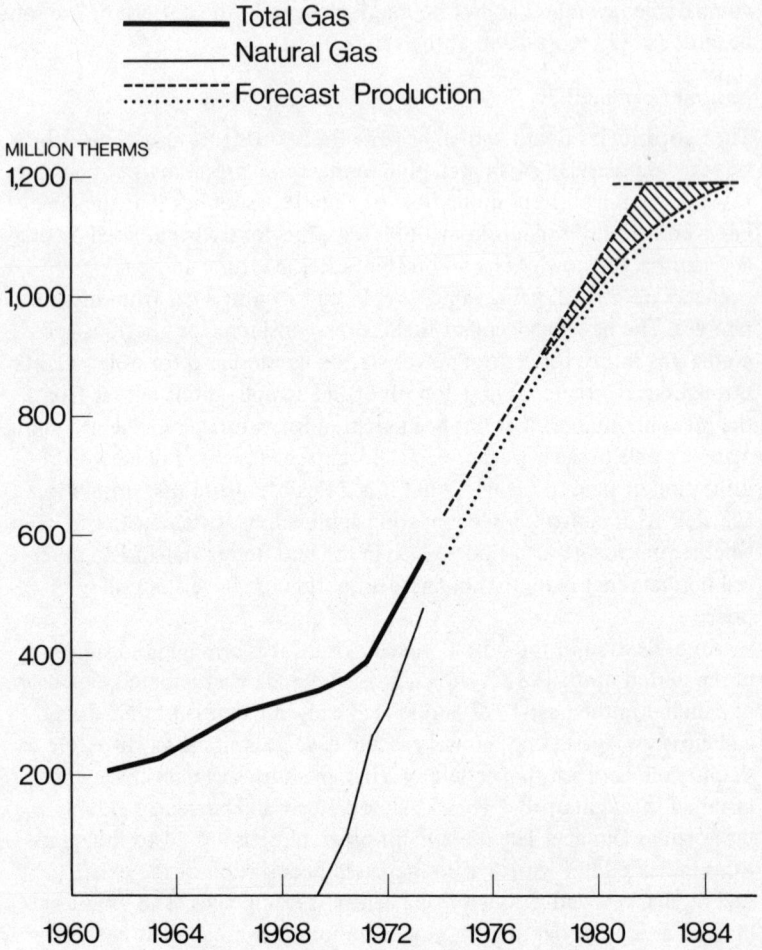

Figure 3. Gas production for Scottish market.

that under existing allowable cost arrangements a price increase of around ten per cent to domestic consumers will shortly be submitted to the Government. The current assessment of the total British market from 1974 to 1975 stands at 4,000 million cubic feet of gas supplied per day. By 1980, the amount should have risen to 6,000 million cubic feet per day, with the increase being largely underwritten by supplies from the Frigg field and additional quantities of associated gas from the East Shetland basin. Production at the Frigg field is expected to reach a 1978 average of 1,400 million cubic feet per day (13.7 milliard Nm3 per year) of gas, and in addition 60,000 to 90,000 tons per year condensate will be delivered to the St. Fergus terminal. Since the field straddles the median line between the UK and the Norwegian sectors, it has been calculated that at least sixty per cent of this production will come from the Norwegian side. The British part of the Frigg field lies in block 10/1, which is owned by the TOM group:

Elf Oil Exploration and Production . . . . 44.45 per cent

Total Oil Marine Ltd. . . . . 33.33 .. .. ..

Aquitaine Oil (UK) Ltd. . . . . 22.22 .. .. ..

While all companies that find gas on the British Continental Shelf are bound by law to offer this to the British Gas Corporation, a unitisation agreement has come into force over the Frigg field. The main agreement between the licensees (the TOM group on the British side, the Petronord group including Statoil on the Norwegian side) is that the gas resevoir will be produced jointly and that Elf Norge A/S will be the common operator. According to the agreement between British Gas and the two groups, gas production from the field will start at the end of 1976 (with a certain flexibility to allow for possible technical delays), and will gradually increase over a period of 2 years until the daily rate reaches 1/5000 of the recoverable reserves. This will correspond to an exploitation period over more than 15 years.

Contracts in connection with pipelaying work for the first pipeline were negotiated on behalf of the British group for the 1974 and 1975 seasons. The Norwegian group has planned that their line will be laid in the 1975 and 1976 seasons, so that for the sale of the gas from the joint field, one line will be available from the start of 1976 and two lines will be available from the Autumn of 1976. The pipe dimensions chosen for both lines conform to an outer diameter of 32 inches and a wall thickness of 0.75 inches. It has also been decided that in the period prior to the second pipeline becoming available, both groups can deliver quantities of gas in proportion to their share in the reserves without any regard to the ownership of the pipeline. With plans for Frigg production already well

advanced, the recent announcement that a major gas pipeline from the
Brent system (operated by the Shell-Esso partnership) will also find a
landfall at the St. Fergus terminal. The Brent field has one of the highest
gas/oil ratios so far encountered in the northern North Sea at over 2,000
cubic feet per barrel of oil output. While the output of associated gas
will in this instance conform to the oil production profile, it is estimated
that 500 to 600 million cubic feet per day should be available. This will
be the first occasion on which the British Gas Corporation has negotiated
the purchase of associated gas rather than supplies from natural gas fields
as in the case of Frigg and the southern North Sea reserves. The laying of
a pipeline, at least 20 inches in diameter, over a distance of around 300
miles in deep water will necessarily be a high cost investment, probably
in the region of £200 million. With St. Fergus as the principal terminal
point for distribution in the national gas grid, it is conceivable that the
pipeline from Brent could act as a main artery in the handling of associated gas from other fields that could be linked to it through spur-line
connections. Undoubtedly the problems of laying a larger diameter pipeline in deep water will be resolved, but the final production potential
will be determined by the gas/oil ratios of any further discoveries in the
northern sector of the North Sea.

While these developments are under way, some Scottish gas consumers have become the first in the world to use a substitute 'natural
gas'. The new gas, which comes from the Westfield works of Scottish
Gas, has been made at a methanation plant which takes low heating grade
gas made from coal and turns it into one composed mainly of methane.
The methanation plant was built to demonstrate the feasibility of the
process on a commercial scale, and has recently been in use for a project
sponsored by a group of US companies headed by the Continental Oil
Company of Oklahoma. While there are plans for the process to be further developed at installations in New Mexico, the Westfield project is
under competitive pressure from North Sea sources and seems likely to
be discontinued. An overall view of the natural gas supply situation
would therefore appear to favour the Scottish market to the extent that
a much greater dependency on this fuel is assured in the period up to
1982 and beyond. From 1973 to 1974, the total gas sales to Scottish
consumers corresponded to approximately 160 million cubic feet per
day; the prospect of an expanding market leads to a figure of around
325 million cubic feet per day in 1982. From the figures already quoted
above it would seem clear that in the region of 16 per cent of the
currently declared production potential of the Frigg and associated gas
fields landed at St. Fergus would satisfy the Scottish market in 1982.

An additional and complicated feature of the Scottish gas market in the intervening period will be the availability of associated gas from the Forties field which will be separated at the Grangemouth refinery. It has already been announced that the total availability of gas at a flow rate of 400,000 b/d of oil is approximately 230,000 tons per year dry gas (largely methane), 430,000 tons per year propane, 280,000 tons per year butane and 100,000 tons per year of condensate. The company states that the disposal of these various streams—whether they should be sold or used as fuel and feedstock for the refinery and chemical plants—is still under evaluation. The methane component alone which is equivalent to 33 million cubic feet per day would correspond to a significant one fifth of Scottish domestic demand at the present time.

Nuclear Electricity

While it is true that the two Scottish Electricity Boards operate a joint generating account with a considerable degree of interconnection capacity with supplies in England and Wales, when nuclear electricity is considered as a primary input to the fuel economy, Scotland is virtually a self-contained entity. The South of Scotland Electricity Board's nuclear generating station at Hunterston on the Ayrshire coast was one of the first three civil stations to be built under the Government's nuclear power programme of 1957. The twin magnox reactors are rated at 570 MW(Th), 160 MW(e) corresponding to a nominal design output of 300 MW, but early operating experience indicated that high load factor (ca. 80%) coupled to improvements in the fuel management schemes could lead to peak generating capacities in the range 360-384 MW. At present, a second nuclear power plant is under construction at the Hunterston 'B' site, adjacent to the first generation reactors. The two new Advanced Gas-cooled Reactors (AGRs) will have a combined output of 1320 MW(e); the first 1 x 660 MW set is due for commissioning in 1974 and the second set in 1975. This will bring the nuclear component to normal twenty per cent of installed generating capacity in the SSEB area.

In addition to the major increase in the nuclear capability of the SSEB, there is also a substantial change in the supply pattern from reactors owned and operated by the United Kingdom Atomic Energy Authority in Scotland. However, the one constant factor on this account appears to be the supply generated by the Chaplecross reactors at Annan; the four reactors were commissioned in 1959, each reactor having a net output rating of 45-47 MW(e), and in recent years, almost the total output from this plant has been sold directly to the SSEB. The principal changes are in the area covered by the North of Scotland Hydroelectric Board and which obviously include the various stages of fast reactor development at Dounreay, Caithness. The experimental fast reactor (DFR) was commissioned in 1959 and has provided a maximum of ca. 5 MW(e) capacity at various times; as this is an experimental assembly the output cannot be guaranteed. On the other hand, a contract may be negotiated for the purchase of the whole of the output from the 250 MW(e) prototype fast reactor (PFR), which is in the final stages of its commissioning period and will be raised to full power during 1975.

On this basis, the maximum installed nuclear capacity available to the Scottish Boards between 1978 and 1982 would be 2134 MW(e). It can be seen from Figure 4 that the potential contribution from the planned output for the 1974 to 1982 period will fall within a very wide band dwarfing the present contribution from both nuclear and hydroelectric sources. Since the pattern of electricity generation throughout the UK will favour high merit nuclear plants at the expense of both oil-fired and coal-burning stations, it is reasonable to assume a very high load factor for the new additions to the installed capacity. The calculated load factor for the period 1970 to 1974 is 78 per cent for existing nuclear stations; if it is assumed that this level of output can be sustained, then at least 14,600 GWn per year could be supplied from 1978 onwards.

There are undoubtedly further prospects for the expansion of nuclear electricity generation in Scotland, although it may prove increasingly difficult to justify the demand forecasts. In a report of the Nuclear Power Advisory Board (Cmnd. 5731) published in September 1974, the demand forecasts for the electricity industry in Scotland incorporate an average growth of demand on the system of 5.9 per cent. This was endorsed by the Scottish Economic Planning Department as historically correct and likely to be maintained by developments arising from North Sea oil. This assumption has then been combined with alternative views of the recovery rate of the British economy in the period after 1975, e.g. the lowest estimate corresponds to the average long term rate of growth of GDP over the last 25 years—about 2.7 per cent—with electricity demand growing at 3.6 per cent. Set against current demands, the build-up of capacity would then take the following form:

Demand (Gigawatts, GW)

	1974/75	1980/81	1985/86	1990/91
England and Wales	45.5	56.7	67.3	84.1
Scottish Boards	6.4	9.1	11.9	15.8
	51.9	65.8	79.2	99.9

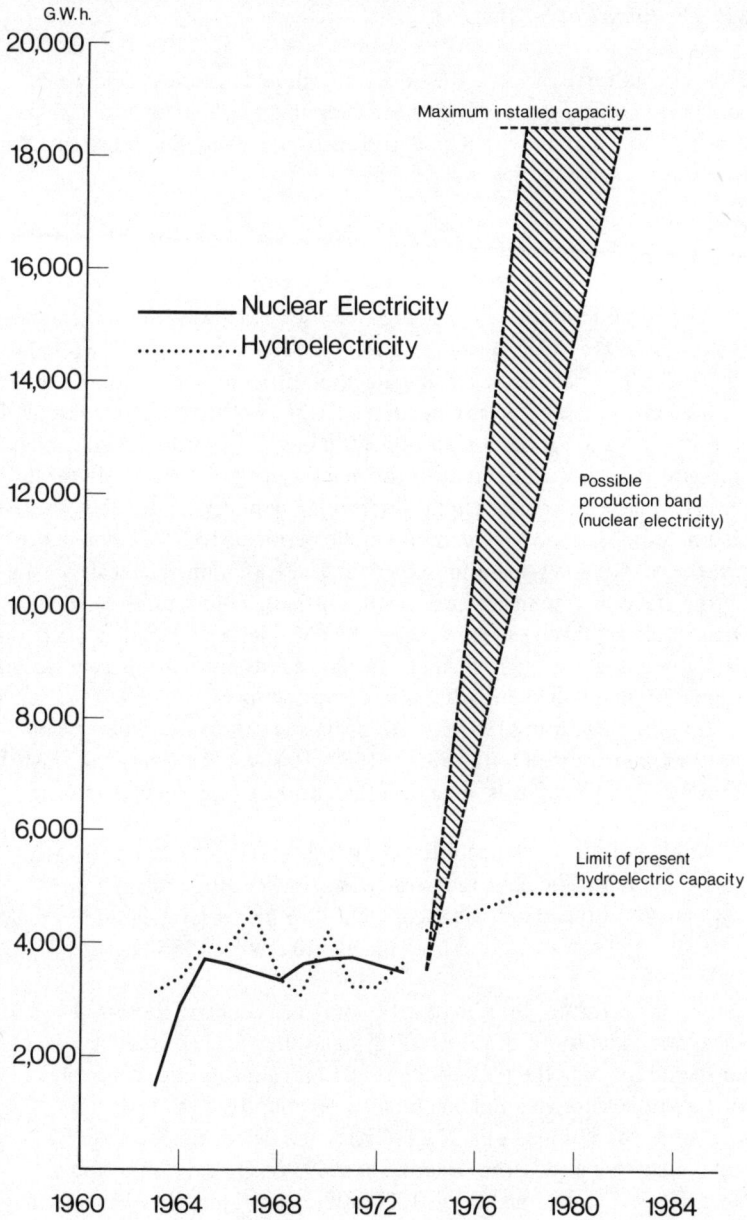

Figure 4. Nuclear and hydroelectricity output.

The demand forecasts have then been interpreted in terms of new capacity requirements after allowing for scrapping of old plant and a 20 per cent planning margin. For the Scottish Boards, this results in incremental additions to capacity beyond 1981 and 1982:

GW	*1981/82-1985/86*	*1986/87-1990/91*	*Total*
Scottish Boards	3.3	5.3	8.6

The SSEB have made a particular case for embarking upon the construction of the Steam Generating Heavy Water Reactor (SGHWR), since there would appear to be no fundamental difficulties in clearing a design of the same general type as that submitted in 1971 for the Stakeness tender for the North of Scotland Hydro-Electric Board. Government policy has subsequently moved in this direction and the design for a 660 MW(e) unit has also been consolidated in the intervening period; despite the aggressive estimates of demand for electricity in the period up to 1982, there is little chance of obtaining operating experience with a commercial scale version of the SGHWR system before 1981/82. Although the viability of the nuclear industry, taken over the country as a whole, is now at stake, in Scotland there is no prospect of any immediate additions to the present nuclear capability that will change the supply position much before 1982. Even a station ordered during 1975 for a location such as Torness Point would not be commissioned until 1981 or 1982. This would appear to be the next prospect if the SSEB reasoning over the future reactor policy is upheld.

SSEB suggest for the country as a whole about 5.0 GW of 660 MW reactors over the next four years. They believe the risks in a programme of this size to be acceptable. The first reactor should in their view be in service by 1981-82 and all 5.0 GW by 1985-86.

On this occasion, the CEGB is far more cautious in assessing the long-term viability of the SGHWR System; they advance the view that to avoid repeating the risks encountered in scaling up the Windscale prototype reactor to a full commercial version, it is first necessary to guarantee the viability of a 1320 MW(e) core design for SGHWR. They argue that to justify series ordering in the 1980s based on the larger unit size, a first demonstration 1320 MW(e) plant might be ordered in 1976 with target commissioning in 1982. Whichever view prevails, there is very little doubt that the escalating price of fossil fuels is likely to increase further the competitive position of nuclear power for base-load generation throughout the country. The supply position in Scotland of nuclear electricity suggests that the major growth taken with the Hunterston 'B' decision will be further consolidated in the next round of power station orders. Both North Sea oil and gas can command premium markets and there would appear to be no economic case (quite apart from thermal inefficiencies of central power stations) to justify their use in firing boiler plant on this scale. Nevertheless the balance between base-load nuclear stations and the more decentralised systems of heat-to-electricity conversion should now be more carefully evaluated. While the latter systems can make no impression on our national balance of payments problem with respect to oil imports in the period up to 1982, they can contribute greatly to optimisation of the fuel mix in power stations over the longer term.

Hydro Electricity

The regular statistical bulletin that is published by the Department of Energy includes the following observation in the November 1974 edition:

> The increase in output capacity during the month includes the commissioning of the first 150 MW set at the North of Scotland Hydro-Electric Board's new pumped storage station at Foyers on Loch Ness. This will be followed by a further 150 MW set which is at present in course of commissioning.

As far as future prospects for hydroelectric power are concerned, this type of system may be the way forward. The official view of the situation in the UK and in Scotland in particular, is that virtually all the hydro resources have been developed. While there are undoubtedly a few possible schemes still remaining, for the most part these are simply not economic at today's interest rates and too small to justify the problems.

It is interesting to note that 1970 was the peak year for electricity generated by hydroelectric stations with an output of 4,282 GWh. Although there is a good chance that this level of output can be sustained in future years, it is still subject to the vagaries of climate. For example, it is worth noting that in 1972 the prevailing weather conditions at that time resulted in a net output of only 3,250 GWh from the same installed capacity. However, the pumped water storage stations at Cruachan at the head of Loch Awe, Argyllshire and now at Foyers on Loch Ness offer a special flexibility and can act to stabilise frequency on the national grid system, particularly during periods of electrical power shortage such as those of recent years.

The North of Scotland Hydroelectric Board draws heavily on the natural water resources of the highland area for the greater part of its generating capacity. At present the distribution of total hydroelectric capacity between the Scottish Boards is as follows:

	NSHEB (MW)	SSEB (MW)
Hydro (conventional)	1,052	–
Pumped storage – Generated	550	124
– Pumped	(600)	(135)

While the northern 'Hydro' Board is recognised as serving a population of 1.25 million in an area of almost 22,000 square miles (57,000 sq. km.), lying west and north of a line from the southern end of Loch Lomond to the Firth of Tay and including the Islands, it does of course include most of the rapidly growing coastal developments concerned with North Sea oil and gas production. In response to this major uprising of economic activity, the Board has invested in a 1,320 MW(e) oil-fired power station at Boddam, near Peterhead. The first 660 MW unit is due to come into operation in 1978, and the second unit a year later. The combined output of this station will alone represent more than one third of the total generation capacity of the Board's power stations, and because of the large fuel oil burn will contribute to stabilisation of the market for petroleum fuels. This must represent a point of departure as far as the Board is concerned and the future investment strategy is therefore more likely to conform to the pattern adopted by the southern Board, which supplies the principal industries and urban consumers in the Scottish central belt.

The Scottish Fuel Economy: an aggregate picture

Although it is extremely difficult to achieve a synthesis of the market positions that might be held by the primary fuels during the coming decade, and never more so than under the present conditions of economic uncertainty, there are sufficient grounds for believing that over this period the energy supply situation in Scotland at least will be considerably more buoyant than the situation over the country as a whole. During the course of this preliminary survey of the current position in each sector of the market, it has been necessary to make certain optimistic assumptions, for example regarding increased mechanisation and productivity from the Scottish coal fields or a stable high load factor for the new generation of nuclear generating plant. In anticipation of the continuing need throughout this period to achieve a reduction in the oil import burden, there will be sustained political pressure to maintain and to improve wherever possible, the overall viability of the coal industry. While there is still evidence for an upward trend in the consumption of petroleum fuels, this is largely sustained by the very large oil-fired power stations that are due to be commissioned at Inverkip and at Peterhead between 1976 and 1980. National balance of payments difficulties could provoke a re-examination of the use of natural gas in the case of Peterhead, although it is widely acknowledged that this would be far from an optimum use for this premium fuel.

If present patterns of consumption continue without radical readjustment, then the aggregate picture that emerges is the one shown in Figure 5. (The data on which this assessment is based are also presented in Table 2.) These figures do not correspond to the final energy delivered to the consumer; it will be noted that while some of the basic fuels are used directly in a wide range of applications, the balance will be taken up by the secondary fuel industries in conversion to other fuels. Consequently, electricity or gas that is generated from coal and oil is not included in this compilation; instead the basic inputs of coal and oil to these processes have been calculated. It seems probable that with the build-up of North Sea oil and gas production there will be a greater flexibility of choice within the general fuel economy to manage the energy requirements of the industrial, commercial and domestic sectors.

Table 2: Primary Fuel Market Scotland 1970-82

						Per cent of total			
		1970	1974	1978	1982	1970	1974	1978	1982
Solid fuels	M tons	13.07	11.26	*12.60	*15.00	42.7	34.3	29.4	30.3
	M therms	3337	2795	3217	3830				
Petroleum	M tons	8.25	9.24	*11.10	*12.00	45.7	48.9	43.6	40.9
	M therms	3572	3978	4783	5171				
Natural gas	M therms	23	561	910	1200	0.3	6.9	8.3	9.5
Nuclear electricity	GWh	3723	3701	14850	18690	4.7	4.4	13.3	14.6
	M therms	366	355	1460	1837				
Hydro electricity	GWh	4282	3853	4930	4930	6.6	5.5	5.4	4.7
	M therms	514	449	592	592				
Net imports of electricity	GWh	−58	+40	—	—				
	M therms	−7	+4						
Aggregate	M therms	7805	8142	10962	1263	100.0	100.0	100.0	100.0

*Mean Values: Solid Fuels—1978/12.60 $\pm$ 0.30, 1982/15.00 $\pm$ 0.60 M Tons
Petroleum —1978/11.10 $\pm$ 0.40, 1982/12.00 $\pm$ 0.80 M Tons

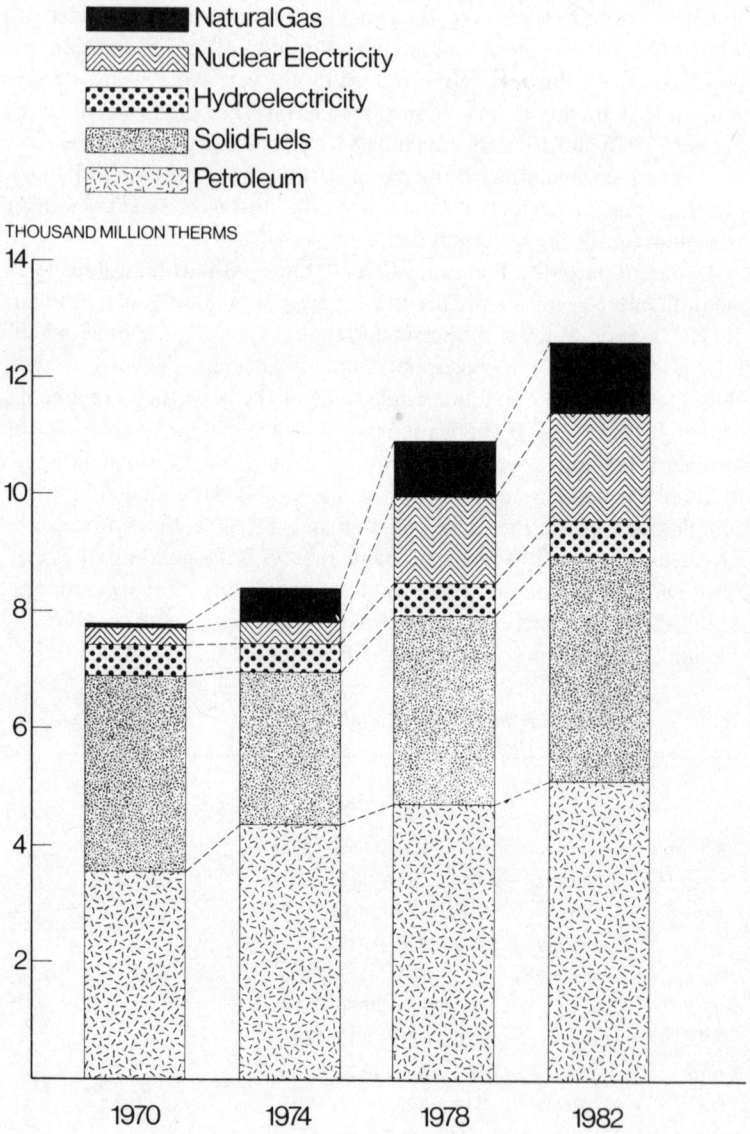

Figure 5. Primary fuel market in Scotland.

In the event of coal production not meeting expectations, then the future significance of natural gas in the overall energy balance will have to be reviewed. If, for example, the level of production in the Scottish coalfields fails to respond to present market conditions, then it is conceivable that coal output, almost exclusively for power generation, could level out in the region of eight million tons per annum. On the 1982 figures, if this deficit was to be covered by the additional production of natural gas, then approximately 1800 million therms would have to be delivered by this industry. While this is probably not realistic from a distribution stand point, it has to be set against the anticipated 325×10^6 cubic feet per day that can now be safely guaranteed to Scottish consumers from North Sea reserves by 1982. The production potential of the giant Frigg field coupled to the associated gas stream from the East Shetland basin is estimated to be around 2000×10^6 cubic feet per day by that time. The additional 1800 million therms, that would need to be produced against the shortfall in coal production, correspond to approximately 490×10^6 cubic feet per day so that a larger fraction of North Sea gas production could almost certainly be accommodated in the Scottish fuel economy than is at present envisaged. This substitution of natural gas for coal has dominated the domestic markets in recent years, and yet remained one of the principal unknowns in view of the comparatively short periods of guaranteed production from offshore fields. Much more detailed studies are necessary to investigate the wide variety of possibilities that are connected with the use and distribution of this valuable fuel.

The approach to the short-term energy supply patterns that has been adopted in this report is obviously quite different to the more usual type of forecasting model. In order to justify future investments of a capital-intensive kind, the energy industry has frequently resorted to projections of demand that are based on expectations of economic growth close to the maximum historical rate. The forecast of the Scottish Electricity Boards, which currently assumes an average growth of the maximum demand on the system of 5.9 per cent, and which is apparently endorsed by the Scottish Economic Planning Department on the grounds that the rate of growth of electricity demand in Scotland has been higher than England and Wales over a considerable period, perfectly illustrates this point. To a certain extent, this problem has been complicated by the lengthy construction period that has now become a feature of planning in this industry. In many cases, the period between tender assessment and final commissioning of the power station can typically extend over a period of six to eight years; with some of the larger nuclear power stations under construction the 'lead' time for construction has been of the order of ten years. For the purpose of the present exercise, it has not been necessary to resort to forecasting procedures that rest on assumptions that will be largely governed by the recovery rate of the British economy once North Sea oil and gas production begins to approach a significant level.

Using this illustration of the heavily time-lagged effects of investment decisions in the electricity supply industry, it is virtually certain that any additional plant ordered during 1975 could not make any substantial contribution to output in 1982. Subject to satisfactory financing arrangements for North Sea developments, most of the critical investment decisions that might influence the calculated energy balance have already been taken. Since the data presented in Table 2 effectively represents the maximum production capability of the Scottish fuel economy in the 1974 to 1982 period, it is reasonable to assume that Government constraints on energy use will probably stabilise demand at some level well within these limits. Some of the possible interactions can, therefore, be tentatively identified:

Switch I: Petroleum to Natural Gas

Active measures to suppress the demand for petroleum fuels have not yet taken root in the general fuel economy of the UK. The Department of Energy statistical returns indicate that the total inland deliveries of refined products in September 1974 were only three per cent below those of September 1973, whereas the Government has been aiming at a ten per cent overall reduction in the 1973 rates. The prospective increases in the Scottish demand for petroleum are almost entirely due to the construction of two large oil-fired power stations (at Inverkip and at Peterhead). A decision to proceed with 'dual-firing' in the case of Peterhead could conceivably result in stabilising petroleum consumption at the 1974 level. On the other hand, more general substitution of natural gas for petroleum-based fuels appears to be already taking place throughout the industrial and commercial sectors with the result that some further price regulation may be necessary in order to protect the premium users. Under the present rather exceptional circumstances in the world oil market, it is possible to view natural gas as a 'bridging' fuel for the UK energy economy rather than as a long-term substitute. It remains to be seen whether any further substantial gas finds in the North Sea would result in a changing attitude to the use of this fuel.

Switch II: Coal to Nuclear Fuel for Electrical Power Generation

It has been mentioned earlier that a considerable fraction of the total coal burnt in Scotland is in central power stations. While the availability of high merit nuclear generating plants will not directly affect the output of electricity from coal-fired stations, it is operationally desirable to avoid power cycling the fuel assemblies in large nuclear reactors. Under these circumstances and with corresponding load factors in the range 75 to 80 per cent, nuclear-based electricity will become increasingly attractive to the Scottish Boards. Rising coal prices will undoubtedly further accelerate the process, and in view of the Government's declared policy on more realistic pricing within the nationalised industries it is difficult to see the coal industry forming any further footholds in the field of electricity production. The production capacity of the coal industry will therefore need to be channelled in other directions if anything approaching the potential 12 to 15 million tons per year is to be realised around 1978 to 1992. In the longer term, the production of synthetic fuels from coal will provide some of the guarantees that the industry is currently seeking.

If the coal burnt in power stations is held at around eight million tons (2040 M therms), petroleum consumption is regulated at 1974 levels, and the other fuels realise their potential as indicated in Table 2, then there is still a planned capacity of 9,647 M therms that will be available in Scotland in 1982. It is under these conditions that the forward provision of energy for the Scottish economy begins to look very encouraging. It is possible to construct a number of hypothetical situations in order to test the strength of the energy supply system in Scotland over this time frame. The present data base is hardly adequate for these purposes, but it does illustrate the advantage of an integrated approach to the energy problem at a regional level. Scotland will inevitably be categorised as an energy-producing sub-system in the national energy model that is at present being evaluated by the Department of Energy. Within the framework of such a regional model, it should be possible to identify and to investigate the specific potential of each primary fuel in contributing to the final energy balance. It is on the basis of this kind of appraisal that future depletion policies and marketing strategies of North Sea gas, in particular, might be decided.

Energy Planning: some Scottish alternatives

One of the very firm recommendations published a year or so ago in a report on economic development and devolution[1] takes the following form:

> the Ministry of Energy of the Scottish Government should have res-
> ponsibilities in two general fields, overall energy policy in Scotland
> and, together with the United Kingdom Government, North Sea oil
> and gas policy.

The authors of this report went for a joint assignment of responsibility
on this controversial subject because they believed that there was a suitable precedent already operating in Scotland, namely that of the Forestry
Commission, which is shared in an administrative sense between the Secretary of State for Scotland and the UK Department of the Environment.
On the other hand, the particular paragraph in the White Paper on
Devolution[2] which refers to the future significance of North Sea oil
revenues reflects a different kind of future:

> There are some who argue that oil revenues should be controlled
> directly by those parts of the United Kingdom off whose shores the
> oil is found, whatever the effect elsewhere. Let there be no misunder-
> standing: such a proposal—whether its advocates realise this or not—
> would mean the break-up of the United Kingdom.

It seems clear that the various positions in this argument will not be
easily reconciled to one another and even a state of compromise, with an
effective sharing of responsibility for the North Sea and for overall energy
policy at a Scottish level, is also not apparently within reach. The official
view remains intransigent; no fragmentation of the energy economy can
take place without an inevitable break-up of the United Kingdom. While
this conflict remains as an area of political deadlock, the important
questions relating to the basis of energy planning in Scotland for the
next ten years are unresolved. In the earlier section, the broad outline
of the development of the Scottish fuel economy has been assessed for
the period up to 1982, and this is more than anything a reflection of
the status quo. It has proved impossible to embark on the type of forecasting exercise that is within the province of the professional energy
planner, namely, to assume that the industrial economy is growing overall at a certain rate, and that the energy sector of the economy is being
pulled along with it. However, the question as to whether the UK energy
economy will go on growing at a little less than two per cent per annum
is merely one of speculation.

By simply evaluating the implications of investment decisions already taken, the picture that has emerged includes some fairly dramatic changes in the energy supply pattern. Around the year 1982, solid fuels will be stabilising at the 30 per cent mark; by this time petroleum fuels will also have fallen back to a 43 per cent market share, natural gas will rise to the region of eight to nine per cent primary energy with nuclear electricity at the level of 13 to 14 per cent and with hydroelectricity retaining a level of four to five per cent. While it does not follow that all of the available energy supply will be fully utilised, the final sum in 1982 does amount to a 55 per cent increase in the potential supply of primary energy available to Scotland. It is reasonable to suppose that Scotland will become an energy-exporting economy. In these circumstances, it is worth considering whether Scotland could benefit as a separately managed energy economy. The problem has been to find any information that can translate the possible alternative supply options that might be made available in Scotland if this was to happen.

A recently publicised report[3] from the Energy Technology Support Unit of the Department of Energy, which has the responsibility for making a UK assessment of alternative energy sources, has reached one tentative set of conclusions. The current integrated total for wind, wave and tidal energy comes out at around 33 mtce which could be topped up with perhaps another 8 mtce according to the deployment of solar heating and geothermal sources. What is impossible to judge is what fraction of these renewable energy resources could be made available in Scotland, and given the normal scale of project finance requirements within the energy industries, whether it might be possible to include smaller production elements of this type in any future system.

Looking at the total across the board, i.e., around 40 million tons of coal equivalent, then it might be possible to put ten to fifteen per cent share or something of that order down to Scotland on the renewable resource account. There are the obvious physiographic and climatic variations across the country, which will make a pronounced difference to these estimates at a regional level; undoubtedly the capacity to refine these calculations will improve with time. Many people would hope that a transformation is already underway whereby changing patterns of energy consumption will result in reducing the demand for primary energy, particularly as far as centralised production is concerned. There is even the suggestion that alternative energy sources could become significant at about the 15 or 20 per cent level of primary energy production in the period up to the year 2000.

Summary

There are major uncertainties governing the supply of energy in Scotland in the period beyond 1982. The period up to 1982 is more or less mapped out and there is basically no way that it can be changed. While the demand for energy may slacken with increasing prices, there is no indication that this will produce any radical changes in the supply base. If demand continues to fall in the short term, then the existing plants would simply be utilised at a lower load factor. There is a possibility, beyond 1982, to introduce prototypes of the alternative energy sources (including solar and wave energy) to offset the large demands which will be made otherwise on the nuclear plant side of the energy balance. At the centre of energy planning in Scotland, there will continue to be major unknown factors, since the UK Government will be reluctant to devolve responsibility for energy planning to a Scottish Assembly.

The most positive thing that can be said at the present time is that there is no real energy supply shortage in Scotland because of the scale of the investment already committed. If a major departure from the existing pattern of fuel dependency was to take place, then this would only take effect in the period after 1982. Efforts to capitalise alternative energy sources will have to be well underway by that time so that by the year 2000 these sources can be seen to contribute at least five per cent of the total primary energy supply. The possibility that this new level of technological innovation exists within the Scottish fuel economy is an exciting prospect for the future.

Notes

1. 'Economic Development and Devolution', Scottish Council Research Institute Ltd., June 1974.
2. 'Our Changing Democracy', Cmnd. 6348, November 1975.
3. 'Alternative Energy Sources', *Atom*, January 1976.

5 THE SCOTTISH DIET

Kenneth Blaxter

There are many misconceptions about the extent of regional differences
in food consumption habits in the United Kingdom. The Yorkshireman
does not exist on a diet of faggots and Yorkshire pudding, the Lancastrian
does not consume an enormous proportion of the energy he needs in the
form of hot-pot and the Cornishman does eat other things than the traditional pastie and clotted cream. Similarly, haggis, neeps, brose, stovies,
porridge and other traditional foods washed down with malt whisky
hardly constitute an habitual diet in Scotland. In fact, the Scots diet is
broadly very similar to that consumed in the rest of the country, and,
probably as a result of the continuing growth of the food processing
industry will become more so as the years pass. There are, however,
some differences between the average diets of the Scots and those of
the English. These can be discerned from the reports of the continuing
survey of the British diet made by the National Food Survey Committee
of the Ministry of Agriculture, Fisheries and Food.

Table 1 makes a comparison between the average diet of the Scots
and the population of the south-east corner of England, including London,
an area which probably deviates most from the general average for England and Wales. The table shows the outstanding difference to be that
the Scots eat 30 per cent less fruit and over 20 per cent more cereal
products than do those in southern England. The table simply gives
broad categories of food and tends to obscure a number of other differences. Thus, within the broad category 'vegetables' the Scots eat 30 per
cent more potatoes but 70 per cent less frozen peas, beans and other
vegetables packed in this convenient way. Again, in the category 'cereals'
the Scots consume 47 per cent more bread but 58 per cent less flour than
do the families in the south, statistics which do not suggest that the Scottish housewife does as much home-baking as her counterpart in the south.
Well over 80 per cent of bread purchased in Scotland is sliced; in England
only about half is pre-prepared in this way. The Scots eat nearly three
times as much canned soup as the English and buy 50 per cent more pre-
cooked and canned meat. These differences in the average diet probably
reflect relative affluence rather than culinary competence; indeed, comparison of the diets in the two regions with the spectrum of diets revealed
by classifications based on social class indicates an economic basis for the

disparity. These days the exercise of home-cooking seems to be a mark of affluence rather than a demonstration of frugality.

Table 1: Quantities of Foods in Major Categories Consumed by Households in Scotland and in south-east England (ounces/person/week unless otherwise stated)

Category	Scotland (a)	SE England (b)	Ratio a/b
Milk and cheese[a]	9.2	10.19	0.91
Meat	35.0	36.7	0.95
Fish	4.8	4.7	1.02
Eggs[b]	4.5	4.2	1.07
Fats	10.5	10.5	1.00
Sugar and preserves	14.9	15.2	0.99
Vegetables	82.5	83.2	0.99
Fruit	20.6	29.9	0.69
Cereal products	64.0	52.2	1.23

Source: 'Household Food Consumption and Expenditure 1973', HMSO 1975.
a Pints of milk equivalent.
b Number.

The amounts of nutritional essentials which the average Scottish diet provides are very similar to those provided in England. The Scottish diet contains very slightly less protein of animal origin, but this is the only major difference discernible from Table 2. As an average diet it is entirely adequate in terms of preventing those deficiency maladies attributable to a lack of particular essentials. However, vitamin D supplies in Scotland are not adequate to meet dietary needs, and in this respect it is known that rickets—the Glasgow disease—has emerged in minority immigrant communities in the larger cities. Sunshine, of course, provides through irradiation much of the vitamin D we need and the incidence of rickets may well reflect the difficulties of immigrants in adjusting to a new environment.

The fact that the diet of the Scots provides adequate amounts of dietary essentials does not, however, mean that it is ideal, nor for that matter is the diet of those in south-east England. There is increasing evidence that components of diet have effects on health other than through the mechanisms of what has been called a hidden hunger. In the long term the diet habitually consumed during early life has been associated with the incidence of a number of diseases of the middle and later years of life.

Table 2: The Nutrients Provided by the Average Scottish Diet and that of the Population of south-east England*

Category		Scotland (a)	SE England (b)	Ratio a/b
Energy	MJ/day	9.8	9.6	1.03
Total protein	g/day	71.5	70.0	1.02
Animal protein	g/day	42.4	45.4	0.93
Fat	g/day	105	109	0.96
Carbohydrate	g/day	298	275	1.08
Calcium	mg/day	980	1030	0.95
Saturated fat	g/day	48.6	51.4	0.95
Unsaturated fat	g/day	11.0	10.8	1.02
Percentage of dietary energy derived from		%	%	
Protein		12.2	12.2	—
Fat		40.1	42.8	—
Carbohydrate		47.7	45.0	—

Source: 'Household Food Consumption and Expenditure 1973', HMSO 1975.

There is epidemiological evidence, not entirely free from criticism, to link the consumption of large amounts of fat and particularly of saturated fat to the incidence of cardiovascular disease. There is a similar positive correlation between the incidence of cardiovascular disease and the consumption of refined sugar—sucrose. There is good evidence that an increased consumption of vegetable fibre in fruits, vegetables and low extraction rate flours reduces the concentration of cholesterol in the blood plasma. High plasma cholesterol has been shown in Western societies to be correlated with increased mortality from ischaemic heart disease. High sugar content and low fibre content of diets have been criticised in other ways. Association of a high sucrose consumption with dental caries is well documented and there is evidence to suggest, but not to prove, that low fibre diets are associated with a high incidence of colonic cancer.

Certainly the normal diet now contains more fat, more saturated fat, more sucrose and less fibre than it did fifty or so years ago. It is equally certain that the incidence of cardiovascular disease and of cancer has increased during this interval and this increase is true even when mortality is related to age classes rather than to the whole community. Whether such a superficial association is more than chance, more than a reflection of concomitant and unrelated changes with time or whether it reflects deeper causal pathways is still conjectural. It is unlikely that the uncertainty could be resolved by direct experimentation, for such experiment would involve decades of the life of man. Understandably many think the strength of the circumstantial evidence such that we cannot afford to await absolute and incontrovertible proof. Several authorities throughout the world, including the Royal College of Physicians have stated that the evidence of association of saturated fat with the incidence of cardiovascular disease is sufficient to warrant its classification as a risk factor and to advise individuals to abstain from eating certain foods and to eat others. The government of Norway in an unprecedented statement has shown its intent to adjust its agricultural policy so as to reduce the proportion of fat in the diet from its present 42 per cent to 35 per cent, replace fats with carbohydrates from cereals and potatoes, increase the proportional contribution of polyunsaturated acids to the total fat supply and reduce the consumption of sugar. The policy was approved by the Storting on 7 November 1975 and received Royal decree on the same day.

Norway is a small country—similar to Scotland in many ways. She has taken a decision about what she thinks the broad attributes of the national diet should be; with the wealth accruing from her North Sea oil deposits she can put such a policy into effect, a difficult matter since to change the pattern of the agriculture and fisheries industries creates vast social change and incurs considerable economic cost. It is reasonable to ask whether the United Kingdom as a whole could emulate Norway's example. The major difficulty of such a step relates to scale, for to obtain a consensus from 55 million people is rather different from gaining the informed agreement of four million. In addition, we are now members of the European Economic Community of 255 million people of widely different living standards, and in which we subscribe to a Common Agricultural Policy. The constraints on a gearing of the United Kingdom's agricultural and food import policy to a national nutritional plan is thus increasingly difficult for, in decision making in Brussels the United Kingdom's voice is but one in nine. The United Kingdom depends on import for 50 per cent of its food supply and is not very good at paying for it and when the objective of the EEC is self-sufficiency in commodities within the market, there is little room for manoeuvre on the part of one member country.

The possibility of Scotland rather than the UK as a whole emulating Norway and linking a nutritional policy to an agricultural policy might appear even more difficult and remote. Yet it seems sensible for any community to safeguard and control the abundance and quality of its food supply. Crucial to such a statement is the definition of community. Idealists argue with my distinguished predecessor, Lord Boyd Orr, that the whole world is the community we must consider, a view echoed at the World Food Conference last year. Others argue that the developing countries must learn to feed themselves rather than depend on the benevolence of those with surplus food or wealth, or must buy food in exchange for raw materials or the products of industrial cropping. One can indeed ask how far this latter division of labour should proceed in the world if this results in an unacceptable dependence and a loss of community identity. No one would suggest that the Kingdom of Fife should be self-sufficient in food, for it is part of Scotland, of Britain and of the United Kingdom and the people identify with one or other community. In the United Kingdom as a whole, however, it is abundantly clear that there has not been a whole hearted acceptance of the idea that our United Kingdom food supply and its quality is now irrelevant in the context of the supra-nationalism of Europe, that in a European division of labour we contribute certain skills in return for food. Perhaps the community we should think about in safeguarding and improving our food supply is that which identifies itself.

Scotland identifies in this way, and we can at least ask about the extent of our self-sufficiency in food and how Scottish agriculture might accommodate agreed changes in a national diet, whether Scotland has the ability as part of the United Kingdom or of the European Community to make such a change or not.

To estimate the proportion of home-produced food consumed in Scotland involves a number of assumptions in instances where there is no separation of the statistical information on Scotland from that on the rest of Britain, and entails careful analysis of information culled from different sources. The methods employed here are given in an extensive footnote to Table 3 where the estimates of primary commodities required are compared with estimates of those produced. The ratios of the one to the other represent self-sufficiencies in commodities and, with one or two exceptions, agree reasonably with estimates made by HM Secretary of State for Scotland in reply to a parliamentary question. They differ considerably more from those estimated by the Edinburgh Junior Chamber of Commerce (1976) who employed a largely financial approach. The results are summarised in Table 3. Scotland produces enough for its own needs, often with considerable quantities to spare of milk and most milk products, beef, mutton, lamb, offal, poultry meat, potatoes, fish and the barley required for beer and spirits. There is about 70 per cent self-sufficiency for pork, bacon, ham and eggs, only about a quarter for cereals, vegetables and butter, and lacking both an oilseed industry and a sugar beet industry, no vegetable-based fat or sugar are produced at all.

Table 3: Estimated Self-Sufficiency of Scotland in Terms of Food Commodities

Commodity	Population requirement in terms of food entering tons x 10^3 [a]	Conversion factor to estimate agricultural equivalent [b]	Estimated requirement (a) tons x 10^3 unless otherwise stated	Estimated agricultural output (b) tons x 10^3 unless otherwise stated [c]	Self-sufficiency ratio a/b
Liquid milk, cream and cheese (solids)	122	12.5% solids	219×10^6 gall	275×10^6 gall	1.26
Beef	133	0.83	$160+13$ [e]	192	1.11
Mutton and lamb	22	0.84	26	57	2.19
Pork, bacon and ham	66	0.85 [d]	$78+8$ [e]	60	0.70
Offal	14	1.00	14	17	1.21
Canned meat	17	0.80	21 [e]	Nil	—
Poultry meat	29	0.70	41	60	1.46
Eggs (number)	1.44×10^6	1.00	1.44×10^6	1.021×10^6	0.71
Butter	36	0.47 lb/gall milk	171×10^6 gall	36×10^6 gall (actual)	0.21
				55×10^6 gall (potential)	0.32
Margarine	30	1.00	30 ⟩	10 [i]	0.12
Lard and other fats	21 + 35	1.00	56 ⟩		
Sugar	243	1.00	243	Nil	—
Fruit	241	1.00	241	18	0.07
Pulses	30	1.00	30	27	0.90
Potatoes	556	1.00	556	550	0.99
Other vegetables	241	1.00	241	55	0.23
Cereals	410	0.72	569	154 [g]	0.27
Fish	43	1.00 [h]	43	233	5.41
Beer [f]	130×10^6 gall	1240 gall/ton barley	104 (barley)	364	3.50
Spirits [f]	3.06×10^6 proof gall	100 proof gall/ton barley	31 (barley)	109	3.51

Notes

a   From the National Food Survey (1975) the ratio of the mean weekly consumption of foods in Scotland to that in the UK as a whole was obtained. This was then applied to estimates of the National supplies of principal foods moving into consumption (see Trade and Industry, 16, no. 10, pp. 512-518, 1974), to arrive at an estimate of the amount of foodstuffs required per head of the population in a year. The population of Scotland was taken to be 5.2 million. This method assumes that the pattern of foodstuffs consumed in catering establishments in Scotland is similar to that in households and bears the same relationship as in the UK as a whole, for the 'food entering' estimate includes catering establishments and manufacture of confectionary and soft drinks while the household food survey excludes these uses (see Household Food Consumption and Expenditure Survey, 1967, HMSO 1969). The estimates of consumption of beer and whisky in Scotland were derived from UK totals in proportion to the population. This is probably an underestimate for whisky especially but no more reliable estimate can be arrived at.

b   The factors derive from published conversion factors (see MAFF 1975) from information obtained from the industries concerned, and from knowledge of the manufacturing processes.

c   These were largely obtained from the estimates 'Scottish Agriculture—Output and Expenditure' (Scottish Agricultural Economics, 25, p. 419, HMSO 1975). The estimate of offal output which is not recorded in the above derives from the ratio of carcass meat/offal for the UK. That for whisky from the Statistical Report Scotch Whisky Association; Edinburgh (1975). There are two estimates for output of butter. The first is based on the estimated amount of milk surplus to needs for liquid milk, cream and cheese manufacture, the other from the actual production of butter as reported by the Milk Marketing Boards in Scotland. The discrepancy indicates that currently milk supplies could support more butter manufacture rather than an excess cheese production.

d   Weighted mean of separate factors for pork and bacon.

e   The requirement of canned meat has been added to the requirement of beef and pig meat in proportion to the requirements of these commodities.

f   The amounts of Scottish barley currently entering the malting and distilling industries is supplemented by considerable quantities of English barley, some North American barley, maize and also by imports of malt. The current production of 182×10^6 proof gallons of whisky is largely destined for export, some 80-85 per cent of the output being exported. The self-sufficiency figure refers to Scottish barley and Scottish estimated requirement.

g   The output includes barley for pearl barley manufacture and oats to be milled for human consumption. The amounts are relatively small.

h   The edible parts are referred to landed weight (i.e. gutted with head on) (see Torry Advisory Note No. 17 HMSO). Output data are from Scottish Sea Fisheries Statistical Tables 1974, HMSO 1975, namely 9.394 x 10 cwt. Between 45 and 50 per cent of this catch is converted to fishmeal. The final figure is fish for human consumption, using 50 per cent of the total catch.

i   Based on an estimate of 8.5 and 10^3 tons of fish oil produced for margarine manufacture.

However, this is not the whole story. The agricultural industry produces commodities in addition to the surplus food products evident in Table 3 and which are exported, mostly to England. These consist of seed potatoes, store cattle and sheep, breeding stock, day-old chicks, hatching eggs and a variety of other intermediates in the farming industry. The wool crop in Scotland is not inconsiderable and of the total Scottish fish catch some 45 to 50 per cent is converted to meal, much of which is exported. Scotland in return imports oilseed cakes and meals and some coarse grains for livestock. It can be asked if what we earn from these agricultural exports and from the surplus feed is sufficient to pay for the wheat, sugar, fats and fruit which are imported. Such an accounting can only be very rough, but at least begins to answer the question whether the food supply of the people in Scotland is grossly supported by the export-related earnings of its industrial sectors.

The calculations shown in Table 4 indicate that Scotland achieves a food balance or close to it as a result of the efforts of her farmers and fisherfolk alone, for the discrepancy of £40 million is small relative to Scotland's gross domestic product of £4,600 million. The export of meat, livestock products and seed potatoes to the rest of the United Kingdom provides revenue to finance the import of sugar and wheat grain and the additional eggs and pig meat currently needed. The fisheries industries and the component of the malting and distilling industries which depend on Scottish barley provide revenue that almost covers the remainder.

Table 4: A Financial Balance Sheet for Food in Scotland: imports by Scotland, exports of farm goods and presumptive export of agriculture and fisheries products surplus to Scotland's domestic needs

Commodity or 'service'	Quantity tons x 10^3	Value of unit	Total value £ x 10^6
Feed commodity needs to meet that part of Scotland's need not met by home production[a]			
Pork, bacon & ham	25	£500/ton	12.5
Eggs (number)	0.21×10^6	£46/1000	9.7
Fats	100	£440/ton	44.0
Sugar	243	£170/ton	41.3
Fruit	223	£120/ton	26.8
Vegetables	185	£90/ton	16.7
Grain	415	£75/ton	31.1
		Total	182.1

Excess food exported to England or elsewhere and export of animals, seed, etc.[b]

Store cattle and sheep			21.2
Breeding animals, game, etc.			7.1
Hatching eggs & other products			1.7
Seed potatoes	274	£50/ton	13.7
Exported barley	40	£60/ton	2.4
Beef	19	£750/ton	14.3
Mutton & lamb	31	£700/ton	21.7
Offal	3	£750/ton	2.3
Poultry	21	£475/ton	10.0
Excess barley[c]	40	£60/ton	26.3
Fish[d]	190	£140/ton	26.6
		Total	147.3

Notes

a   The quantities derive from the deficits in home production in Table 3. All fats—butter, margarine, cooking fat, lard and fat incorporated into prepared dishes have been totalled; the value of unit product which is based on the wholesale price of butter is probably too high. The fruit entry includes all fruit including imported citrus fruit. The average price derives from the mean price to the producer of culinary and dessert apples. With vegetables the cost per unit derives from cauliflowers; it is probably too high as an average. The price of wheat has been taken to apply to all cereals including maize and rice.

b   The first three entries are those of Table 256 in Scottish Agricultural Economics, 25, No. 10, p. 421. The seed potato entry is the amount of seed sold and will include some Scottish purchase. The price has been taken as 2 x the ware price in 1974-5 rather than the grossly inflated price in the current planting season. The exported barley is the actual grain export. Cattle and sheep meat prices are mean returns to producers, corrected in the case of beef for a killing-out percentage of 55.

c   The amount of barley in Scotland entering the malting and distilling trades is grossly in excess of the amount of barley needed to provide beer and spirits for the Scottish people. Rather than cost this excess barley in terms of beer and whisky—entailing an added value—the barley has been costed at ex farm price.

d   The value of the total Scottish fishing catch and shellfish in 1974 was £64.1 million; the mean value per cwt was £7 or £140 per ton. The catch has been reduced to 50 per cent since that proportion is used to manufacture fishmeal.

The Scots are somewhat vulnerable to external forces since their main energy staples—grain, sugar and fats—have to be imported into the country. They are more vulnerable in this respect than are the people in the rest of the United Kingdom. Thus, home production of sugar in the rest of the UK met 42 per cent of requirement in 1973-74; in Scotland it was and remains zero. With milling wheat, new varieties ensure that the rest of the UK produces 48 per cent of their own needs, but Scotland meets but 27 per cent. The whole of the UK is highly dependent on overseas countries—including in this category European countries—for its fat supply. Vulnerability in this sense means that import is dependent on supply and prices in the world or European markets. Thus, within a year, from 1973 to 1974, there has been an unprecedented rise (more than three-fold) in the world price of sugar, and crop failures in the Soviet Union and elsewhere coupled with changes in cropping policies in the USA have recently created major vagaries in the world price of hard wheats. It might seem reasonable to insure against any future problems of this sort. In view of the association of sugar and fats with cardiovascular disease, however, it might be more sensible to rely on an importation which can be controlled downward if need be. If sugar is expensive, not good for the teeth and possibly a life-shortener, there is no need to buy it in massive amounts and possibly no need to ensure that it is produced expensively at home. A small modern sugar beet industry is, however, a normal safeguard.

I think it would be sensible to increase wheat production, vegetable production and production of dairy produce including butter in Scotland. More important, recognising that about a fifth of Scotland's primary agricultural output caters for needs outside her borders for products which others want, we should expand such enterprises to generate wealth from a farming base. A plea for more wheat, more vegetables and soft fruit, more seed potatoes to the limit of the market and more high quality livestock and livestock products not neglecting Scotch whisky clearly rules out another option or series of them. It has been argued by some that with its magnificent scenery the tourist industry of Scotland could be vastly expanded, and that farming should take a secondary place to the provision of amenity for the people of industrialised England and Europe. While regulated tourism on its present scale is not at variance with farming, the large-scale development of such an industry might well be so. The option of developing a tourist industry to provide revenue for basic necessities does not to my mind provide the safeguards which seem necessary.

Such increases in food production and in the production of export products by Scottish farms will involve new resources and a different deployment of those we already have. The primary resource of land might seem from an atlas quite sufficient, but the breakdown in Table 5 shows that although Scotland has nine per cent of the UK population on 32 per cent of the land area, much of this is hill and mountain with limited potential. Scotland has more agriculturally productive land per head of the population than does England—reflected in the present food self-sufficiency—but this land is not all of first-class quality and its use is limited by the weather. Average temperature is nearly two centigrade degrees lower than that in England, there is 10 per cent less sunshine and 10 per cent more rain, particularly in the West where topography, soil types and high rainfall make arable production difficult. Furthermore, land is being lost to urban and forest development at the rate of 23,000 hs/year. Land improvement to increase agricultural production entails considerable investment.

Table 5: The Land Resources of Scotland and of England and Wales (million acres)

	Scotland	England and Wales	Scotland as a proportion of the UK[a]
Total land area (excluding water)	19.07	37.15	0.32
Cultivated land)	3.08	13.95	0.17
Permanent pasture)	1.02	9.73	0.08
'Crops and grass'	4.10	23.68	0.14
Rough grazings	11.14	4.52	0.69
Population x 10^6	5.2	49.2	0.69
			Ratio: England and Wales: :Scotland
Crops and grass acres/person	0.79	0.48	1:1.64
Effective agricultural land acres/person[b]	1.21	0.50	1:2.42

Source: Annual Abstract of Statistics, HMSO (1975)
a The rough grazings are attributed with an output which is one-fifth that of crops and grass, which are together usually regarded as the agricultural land of the country.
b Includes Northern Ireland.

There are other problems. At present there is no good variety of spring wheat for Scottish conditions; no orchards and no varieties of many vegetables to suit cool summers and with a modicum of frost resistance. Nor are there the central complexes to process such vegetables, though in England they are increasing. Labour is scarce, particularly for fruit and vegetable crops. The labour force in farming has fallen by 35 per cent since 1965 and lack of skilled farm labour is now causing difficulties and indeed dictating farm production patterns in many parts. All in the farming community agree that the remuneration and local community services for rural workers should be increased in order to retain and augment the work force. This, however, necessarily implies price structure for farm produce commensurate with the costs they incur.

To increase agricultural production will certainly entail higher end prices for food since the capital to be invested must be serviced and the income of those who live by the land must be augmented. Increases in food prices are, however, inevitable whatever happens since in the UK as a whole the policy of cheap food is now being superseded, and a modest expansion of Scottish agriculture along the lines suggested, coupled with a reduction of costs of transport of food from the rest of Europe would not necessarily result in a proportionally greater increase than that already anticipated for the UK as a whole.

Nevertheless, increases in the relative price of food from whatever cause raises concern. It has been cogently argued by Dr Passmore that the nutritional poverty of Scotland in the nineteenth century was largely the result of a displacement of the traditional diet—of oatmeal, milk, kale, cabbage, ale and fish, occasionally supplemented with meat—by the cheaper industrial diets of white bread, sugar, unfortified margarine, and tea, supplemented by very few vegetables because of the disappearance of the kale yard. When tea replaced ale and milk as the main beverage of the Scots it was castigated as a 'vile drug' and considered to corrupt morals and debilitate the constitution. The latter may be true since tea provided little if any nutrients to replace those in the milk and ale it replaced. If food prices rise then it is imperative to ensure against a similar nutritional deprivation in some of those less affluent groups of the population. Implicit in such a statement is a still wider interpretation of the view that a community should safeguard the quality and abundance of its food supply. Not only are agricultural and fisheries policies inseparable from a good provision policy, but all are part of a more general social concern. We regard health and education as matters of central concern to the whole community to be removed from the arenas of economic constraint. So too should food be regarded. Food is too important a feature and part of all our lives to be determined by ill-understood economic forces outside our control or planned other than by ourselves.

6 HEALTH CARE

Michael Parry

It is often said that Scotland has a poor health record, but this statement needs considerable qualification. The inference comes from information about the people who live in Scotland, and in particular the ages at which they die and from what causes. Mortality rates are a useful but very crude measure of the prevalence of serious disease, and disease is an important, though not the only, factor in estimating the relative healthiness of a population. In 1972 the number of infants dying in the first year of life was a little higher in Scotland than in England and Wales—188 per 10,000 live births as compared with 172—but this latter rate compares unfavourably with some Scandinavian countries (Table 1).

Table 1: Infant Mortality Rate per 10,000 Live Births 1972*

Scotland	188
England & Wales	172
Finland	121
Denmark	122
Norway	118
Sweden	108

Source: WHO, World Health Statistics Annual for 1972.
* Figures rounded.

The number of deaths occurring among children and young adults was similar in Scotland to that of the rest of the United Kingdom and most Scandinavian and Western European countries, but there is cause for concern in middle age. Seventy-two in each 10,000 people between the ages of 45 and 54 died in Scotland in 1972, as compared with 59 in England and Wales, and only 44 in Norway (Table 2). The position is similar among those aged 55 to 64, 180 dying per 10,000 as compared with 153 in England and Wales, and 108 in Sweden; but again the figure for Finland—164—is high.

Table 2: Mortality Rates per 10,000 Population Aged 45 and Over from all Causes in 1972*

		Deaths per 10,000 population		
Age:	45-54	55-64	65-74	75+
Scotland	72	180	429	1192
England & Wales	59	153	382	1129
Finland	67	164	391	1169
Denmark	55	132	336	998
Norway	44	113	306	1012
Sweden	45	108	293	993

Source: WHO World Health Statistics Annual for 1972.
* Figures rounded.

Part of this difference in mortality can be attributed to the effects of heart disease and lung cancer. This is particularly striking among men. In 1972 there were 32 deaths per 10,000 of the population aged between 45 and 54 from ischaemic heart disease and 91 of those aged 55 to 64 in Scotland, compared with 25 and 71 in England and Wales. The comparable figures for Sweden were less than half these (Table 3). Lung cancer deaths were also disturbing: seven deaths per 10,000 for the 45 to 54 year-olds and 19 for those aged 55 to 64, as compared with 5 and 17 for England and Wales, four times as high as in Sweden (Table 4). These are simply examples from two diseases; death rates from many other causes are higher in Scotland than in England and Wales, and this adverse experience affects people in all walks of life.

Table 3: Mortality Rates per 10,000 Population Aged 45 and Over from Coronary Artery Disease*

		Deaths per 10,000 population		
Age:	45-54	55-64	65-74	75+
Scotland	32	91	241	759
England & Wales	25	71	200	669
Finland	31	87	224	732
Denmark	16	52	166	619
Norway	16	52	167	587
Sweden	14	48	160	633

Source: WHO, Int A List 81-88, World Health Statistics Annual for 1972.
* Figures rounded.

Table 4: Mortality Rates per 10,000 Population Aged 45 and Over from Carcinoma of Trachea, Bronchus and Lung*

	Deaths per 10,000 population			
Age:	45-54	55-64	65-74	75+
Scotland	7	19	31	29
England & Wales	5	17	29	25
Finland	3	13	21	19
Denmark	3	11	20	20
Norway	1	4	8	7
Sweden	1	4	11	12

Source: WHO, Int A List A 51, World Health Statistics Annual for 1972.
* Figures rounded.

The number of deaths attributable to certain causes is only one measure of the health of a population. Many people have heart disease without dying from it, and the death rate does not necessarily reflect the prevalence of a particular disease. Information about the incidence of disease—that is the frequency with which diseases arise during a particular period of time—is far less easy to obtain. Certainly more people are admitted to hospital for treatment, and stay longer, in Scotland than in England and Wales, and general practitioners are consulted more often too. But there are more hospital facilities and a higher proportion of doctors in Scotland than in England and Wales, and it is known that there is a direct relationship between the supply of medical services and their use; a higher rate of consultation does not necessarily mean that there is more sickness—simply that there is more extensive provision of medical services in Scotland. It is not at all easy to find out just what the prevalence of disease is in a community. Records kept in hospitals and in general medical practices tell us very little about the prevalence of diseases for which treatment is not sought and nothing about diseases whose effect has not given the sufferer cause to seek assistance.

The screening of large numbers of people for the presence of disease is an elaborate and expensive business and it is not undertaken without a very specific purpose in mind, for instance X-raying large numbers of people in a search for tuberculosis, the early signs of which are seen radiographically long before the illness reveals itself to the patient. Screening—that is, the specific search for a particular sign or signs of known disease[1] is rarely justifiable except where it is important to apply a specific remedy at an early stage of an illness, and where a reliable test for that disease is available. It would be wholly impracticable to screen a whole population for the presence of all detectable disease, but certain prone groups have been studied by screening methods. For instance, the knowledge that the incidence of ischaemic heart disease in men in their early forties is nearly three times as great in Edinburgh as in Stockholm has led to the study of a random sample of apparently healthy men aged 40 in each city.[2] Certain risk factors known to be associated with ischaemic heart disease were found to be present in more Edinburgh than Stockholm men, and it was significant that there were more cigarette smokers in Edinburgh than in the Stockholm group, since cigarette smoking is known to be associated with ischaemic heart disease.

Studies such as these may lead to a better understanding of why the incidence of some serious or killing diseases is higher in Scotland than elsewhere, and in particular whether there are ethnic or environmental factors—social, physical or psychological—which could account for this. There undoubtedly are such factors. The association between cigarette smoking and ischaemic heart disease and cancer of the lung is widely accepted,[3] but making use of this knowledge for the benefit of the health of the population is not so straightforward as making use of a new therapeutic agent for the treatment of an overt disease. It places an onus upon the patient to care for his own health rather than upon the physician to treat his illness. The same applies when it comes to the reduction of cardiovascular disease, and its association with habits of diet, exercise and other aspects of life style. This is referred to in a recent report from the Royal College of Physicians of London on the causes of coronary heart disease,[4] which it relates to habits of cigarette smoking, exercise and diet. Responsibility for the necessary preventive measures, the College believes, lies partly in the hands of public authorities in their control of food production and catering practices, in providing facilities for leisuretime activities, and in the control of cigarette advertisements. But much, says the College, will rest upon individual people themselves in understanding the nature of the risks that they take.

The major improvement in life expectation and health which has taken place in the past hundred years has been as much due to major social changes—which have reduced urban overcrowding, improved sanitation and personal hygiene and provided safer food and better diets—as to the development of specific treatment for particular diseases. Important though it is, curative medicine is only a part of the business of preserving and improving health. Indeed, health is more than the absence of disease; as the World Health Organization insists, it is a state of complete physical, mental and social wellbeing. Various writers have stressed its varying nature and the capacity of the individual to change his health status in a dynamic way. Hence a healthy individual has been described as:

> a well integrated individual, both as to his physical structure and to his physiological and psychological functioning . . . health is not a condition; it is an adjustment. It is not a state but a process. That process adapts the individual not only to our physical but also to our social environment.[5]

> Health is a state of relative equilibrium of body form and function which results from its successful dynamic adjustment to forces tending to disturb it. It is not a passive interplay between body substance and forces impinging upon it but an active response of body forces working towards re-adjustment.[6]

The evaluation of health has to take into account social and cultural factors as well as the physical and psychological characteristics of individuals. Subjective feelings of wellbeing affect the 'healthiness' of an individual and his capacity to adjust to external circumstances. Health for an office worker is different from health for a deep sea diver. Someone who feels well and can act in a way which satisfies himself and the ordinary demands of society may be considered 'healthy' even though he may have a disease or a significant disability. On the other hand, someone who shows no detectable evidence of a physical illness may be regarded as unhealthy because he feels 'unwell' or cannot hold down a job. The essential factor appears to be successful adaptation, and the capacity to adapt is apparent from the wide variation in the physical and mental attainments of different individuals.

It is the role of the general medical practioner to take into account these many factors, as the Royal College of General Practitioners recognises:

> The general practitioner is a doctor who provides personal, primary and continuing medical care to individuals and their families . . . his diagnosis will be composed in physical, psychological and social terms. He will intervene educationally, preventatively and therapeutically to promote his patients' health.[7]

This is not a new role for the general practitioner; it is a re-statement of the traditional task of a doctor to care for individuals as a whole, and not simply to treat bits of the body that go wrong from time to time. It is not surprising however if doctors have tended to be regarded in recent years as fighters against disease rather than as people who care for others, because advances in the treatment of specific diseases have been so remarkable in the past century. The discovery and mass production of antibiotics have revolutionised the treatment of communicable diseases and their hazard to children and young adults; advances in anaesthesia and surgical techniques have greatly improved the outcome of many acute illnesses and relieved the pain and suffering they cause, and the resources of the National Health Service have brought these services within reach of everyone in this country.

But these and other advances in the relief and cure of specific diseases have shifted the focus of attention from the single dramatic incident to the problems of chronic and degenerative disorder. Such is the armamentarium of modern medicine that the care of any one patient now involves many different skills, the coordination of which poses significant difficulties in medical management. Medicine impinges upon the social as well as the physical environment. Just as doctors in the last century became aware of the ill effects of inadequate sanitation and of atmospheric pollution upon the physical health of their patients, so now they are more and more conscious of the adverse effects of the social environment upon wellbeing, for they are asked to deal with a variety of behavioural problems such as addiction to alcohol, the control of fertility and conflicts within the family. Advances in understanding human biology have to include an understanding of human behaviour and the ways that it can cause illness. It is significant that the Royal Commission on Medical Education, reporting in 1968, laid stress upon the need for the behavioural sciences to be taught to medical undergraduates, reflecting the view of the General Medical Council which a year previously had said:

In the Council's view the study of human structure and function should be combined with the study of human behaviour. The Council considers that instruction should be given in those aspects of the behavioural sciences which are relevant to the study of man as an organism adapting to his social and psychological, no less than to his physical, environment. Instruction in the biology and sociological bases of human behaviour, normal emotional and intellectual growth, and the principles of learning theory should be included.[8]

There is hard evidence that disease processes reduce life expectancy to a greater degree in Scotland than in most other countries of the western world, and there is some less well substantiated evidence that certain chronically disabling diseases are more prevalent there. These diseases have certain associations with habits of diet and of exercise, and, more significantly, with smoking. Little is known about the effects of the physical environment, although there is some evidence that migrant Scots tend towards the mortality of their host country and that migrant English who have moved to Scotland tend to have higher cardiovascular mortality rates. Investigations are also being undertaken about the possible ill effects of the soft water which is characteristic of Scotland, and its association with cardiovascular disease.[9] Alcoholism, which is undoubtedly more of a problem in Scotland than in most countries, is the likely cause of the higher mortality from cirrhosis of the liver, and it may also play a part in other disease processes.

But against this background of apparently greater prevalence of serious disease, absence from work because of sickness is very little different in Scotland from many other parts of the United Kingdom— indeed it is lower than in some—and in the General Household Survey into the extent of longterm illness causing restricted activity, Scotland fared better than most of the United Kingdom. In other words, although Scotland has more than its share in the western world of certain serious life-threatening diseases there is no firm evidence that the health—in the widest sense of the term—of its people as a whole is any worse than in other countries. This does not mean that the health problems of its society are anything but formidable; they are shared in varying degrees with other western countries. Solutions will depend more upon changes in society than on advances in medical knowledge.

In so far as disease contributes to the illhealth of the population in Scotland, the ebb and flow of communicable disease will continue to need vigilance in prevention and prompt specific treatment, particularly in the context of today's rapid means of communication; and there may yet be a serious pandemic caused by microbes against which no remedy is known. Greater cause for concern will however be the disabling processes of chronic disease, the effects of which even the hardiest human frame cannot overcome. The search for causes will continue, with due priority being given to those conditions which cause the early death of the sufferer. But that search is conditioned by the knowledge that the ultimate fate of every human frame is deterioration and death: expectations of longevity are value judgements made partly in the light of the expectations of medical science but partly also of the achievements of society as a whole. Indeed the ingenuity with which medicine prolongs life has in some cases been questioned, and this throws into relief the fundamental issue as to the nature and purpose of life itself.

All doctors face the perplexity of the patient with apparently minimal signs of overt disease, whose age and physical state give reason to expect many years of continued active life, but who nevertheless succumbs to the burden of chronic invalidism or early death. Such patients are in sharp contrast to the lively vigour of those who appear to accept extensive handicap as if it were a challenge to test their ingenuity and to add spice to an exciting and rewarding life. This wide and varied spectrum of overt disease, illness, indisposition and wellbeing opens the way to much potentially rewarding medical activity, notably in the field of early detection of preventable illness and remedial disability; and new measures are needed to direct public attention to medical solutions which are not contained in the bottle of medicine or box of pills, to be consumed as a magic potion to expel an evil spirit.

Health education can too readily be dismissed as the sanctimonious pleadings of pious do-gooders for a straitjacket upon man's *esprit de vie*. Clearly the protagonists of the safety-belt philosophy are not motivated by a desire to curtail man's freedom of action—indeed what greater sacrifice of freedom is there than the prison of physical handicap imposed by the road accident? The fervour of the health educationist is derived from the ineradicable memory of the ravages of self-imposed disease and injury. The key is in education, the acquisition of knowledge which brings enlightenment and the great benefits of intelligent choice. To see a doctor as a sort of repair man for the human frame is a gross misinterpretation of his role as teacher; medicine's greatest contributions to the improvement of human health have been its discoveries of hazards to human life and the means of preventing their effects. Some solutions have been found in social legislation, but further progress rests with each member of the community.

One of the unfortunate by-products of the National Health Service has been a widely held belief that having nationalised health, the state is responsible for it. It is no doubt right that the state should remove much of the financial impediment between an individual and services he may need from the medical profession, but the demand for such services has far exceeded any country's means to pay, with the consequence that the state intervenes to determine health care priorities. It is easy to be persuaded that because certain sections of the community fail to make adequate use of freely available health services and suffer unnecessary hardship and discomfort, therefore the services should be directed to their aid. There is of course no doubt that in allocating limited funds, health authorities must be guided by estimates of need for services which are poorly represented by client demand, taking account of those areas of health care—such as in child, geriatric and mental health services—where needs are often not sought on the patient's own initiative. A balance must be struck between medically-initiated and client-initiated health care; in the enthusiasm for seeking out the prone, exposed or inarticulate individual so that he may benefit from effective medical remedy, the public as a whole must not be encouraged to abdicate from the responsibility which most individuals should bear for their own health.

Not only do people perceive and react to physical symptoms and types of behaviour in different ways, but their response to treatment and preventive measures is also influenced by their culture. A great deal of misconception about the causes of and remedies for illness persists. In a detailed study of the population of two districts of London on the subject of the medicines and measures taken by adults in the management of their health complaints, it was shown[10] that a great many people did treat their own complaints without recourse to medical advice, and that this varied very little among various social groups. There were significant gaps between lay and medical interpretations of the signs and symptoms of disease, and it would seem that there is a widespread need for better understanding by the general public of the early signs of progressive disease, the nature of illness, and its relationship with health.

The rapid growth of scientific medicine and increasing specialisation has somewhat debunked the idealisation of the 'Dr Cameron' type of country practice—'the compleat doctor' as the focus of medical knowledge for his family of patients. Yet the shift of the pattern of disease from the acute incident to a series of episodes during the evolution of chronic disability, calls for a medical service which provides continuity of care over extended periods of time and for special medical skills in balancing the relative effects of disease processes with each individual's particular reaction to ill health. This is the essence of good general practice—the use of sharp diagnostic skills in the early signs of disease, wide knowledge of an individual's personal reaction to illness, and continuity of surveillance of patients. General practitioners have found that the free access by the public to their services has resulted in such a demand for advice and treatment for a wide variety of complaints that there is little opportunity to give adequate time to teach the patient how to identify the medically significant event, or to interpret for himself his own reactions to illness. This has led to significant changes in the organisation of general practice; custom-built premises have been provided with improved diagnostic and treatment facilities; secretarial services have enabled practices to be more efficiently organised and medical records to be improved; and health visitors and nurses have joined their medical colleagues in practice, relieving them of responsibility for many services which do not require a doctor.

These improvements have provided, and are continuing to provide, general practitioners with the opportunity to devote more time to their educative role, but this can be successful only if the public as a whole can adjust its view of the medical consultation so as to see it as a health counselling service as well as a repair service for the human body.

Scotland has become accustomed to looking to a welfare state to provide a remedial health service, and when that fails, expecting it to bear responsibility for the care of the dependent. But where is the state to find the resources to meet the mounting demand from a population whose average age, together with the concomitant burden of chronic and disabling illness, will continue to increase? It has recently become very clear that there is a limit to the resources that can be devoted to health and social services. Recent measures to contain expenditure have called upon health authorities to allot a smaller slice of the cake to the 'acute illness' hospitals in order that more resources can go towards services in the community for those whose needs are less explicitly made known. There is a general assumption that health care needs are predictable, and that the main task is an arrangement of priorities—a shopping list of desirable goodies. Within the conventional model of health care, the future looks gloomy—a future of deteriorating institutions bulging with deteriorating people. But if health is a dynamic process, its boundaries personal to each individual, conformity to prescribed norms defies the use of conventional scientific measures.

Nearly thirty years ago the decision was taken to fund centrally a great variety of health service agencies and institutions. Since then, the institutions in particular have grown at a great pace, driven by astonishing technological advances and medical ingenuity. The aim was to provide all that medicine could offer; but it is now obvious that the conquest of disease is only a part of the attainment of health. The other side of the health coin concerns choices which are substantially for individual people to make.

Scotland has, since the health service was nationalised, had its own service, which is distinguishable from that of England and Wales in a variety of ways. One of these is the noticeably easier relationship between the health care professionals and the health departments; this may be a product of the smaller scale of the service, which facilitates communications, the process of consultation and the free flow of experience and understanding. If this extends to the newly formed local health councils, a further step will have been taken towards establishing the partnership between the governors and the governed and the participation of an informed and understanding public which are the keys to a healthy society.

References

1. *Screening in Medical Care (1968),* Nuffield Provincial Hospitals Trust, OUP, London.

2. Oliver, M.F., Nimmo, I.A., Cooke, M. *et al.* 'Ischaemic Heart Disease and Associated Risk Factors in 40 Year Old Men in Edinburgh and Stockholm'. *Eur. J. Clin. Invest.* 5 (6): 507-4, 21 November 1975.

3. Leading Article, *British Medical Journal* (1976) *2*, 439.

4. Report of a Joint Working Party of the Royal College of Physicians of London and the British Cardiac Society: 'The Prevention of Heart Disease', *JRCP,* 1976, vol. 10, No. 3, April 1976.

5. President's Commission on the Health Needs of the Nation, 'Building America's Health: A Report to the President.' America's Health Status, Needs and Resources (Washington DC: US Government Printing Office, 1952-1953) vol. 2, p. 13.

6. Perkins, W.H. *Cause and Prevention of Disease*, (Lea & Febiger, Philadelphia, 1938).

7. 'The Educational Needs of the Future General Practitioner,' *JRCGP* (1969) *18,* 358.

8. General Medical Council: 'Recommendations as to Basic Medical Education' London, 1967.

9. 'Health Services in Scotland'–Report for 1975, HMSO, Edinburgh, (1976).

10. Wadsworth, M.E.J., Butterfield, W.J.H., and Blaney, R. *Health and Sickness– The Choice of Treatment,* London, Tavistock, (1961).

7 THE EDUCATIONAL SYSTEM

James Scotland

People trying to look into the future generally begin by scanning the past. Some years ago[1] I drew attention to a number of continuing trends in Scottish education. These persisted long enough to be described, reasonably, as traditions, and to hazard any kind of informed guess about the direction of the next two or three decades they must be taken into account, not least because, within the last decade, almost all of them have been seriously questioned.

High on the list is the deference Scotsmen have always paid to the aristocracy of the intellect and the magic power of words, that academic bias which encouraged generations of teachers to devote the majority of their time to their brainier pupils. For a quarter of a century this practice has been under attack because it undervalues practical and aesthetic studies, diverts the schools into a private world remote from everyday life, and makes job training a poor relation unless the job happens to be an academic one. However, there is some recent evidence that even Scotland has been moving away from such intellectualism: the Honours Graduates' Association certainly thinks so, pointing to the increasing amount of attention now paid to non-academic pupils and to the number of prize posts in the teaching profession open even to non-graduates.

A second tradition places the Scottish Education Department firmly at the heart of the educational system and the teacher at the centre of the educational universe, with the use of stern discipline to maintain the arrangement. 'The highest tension of authority', wrote Horace Mann in 1843[2] 'which I anywhere witnessed was in Scottish schools', and a generation ago the primacy, indeed the dictatorship, of the teacher had not been questioned. In the last decade there has been a retreat here too. 'Child-centring', piously approved for half a century, has actually been attempted. The 'doctrine of interest' has been put into practice in many schools. Teachers have been given some freedom to experiment, pupils to state their opinions, however jejune, while Her Majesty's Inspectors have slipped further and further into the background, and the SED has been content to have its way by proffering advice and doling out money. But the process has not gone far, as we may see from incidents like those in Summerhill Academy in Aberdeen, where extremism provoked open conflict and showed how influential conservatism still was.

Scotland has been a poor nation: one has only to drive from Glasgow to London to understand that. The effect has been twofold: on the one hand, enforced parsimony and reduced experiment, on the other, education prized as the golden way up, the traditional road for the lad of parts. In the fifties and sixties the money became available, and experiment became not only permissible but almost mandatory; change was the rule. The recent return to hard times appears to have put the clock back. Here is one tradition, it seems, re-establishing itself: necessity is the mother of authoritarianism.

Most of Scotland's ancient schools, training colleges and universities are religious foundations. Perhaps the most influential man in the old parish school system was the local minister, and when the school boards took over his influence continued as the man best able to combine interest, intelligence and availability. Yet here, evidently, is a tradition with shallow roots: which honest man would claim that Scottish education has a religious bias today?

There is good reason for speaking of such traditions. In a small country, where centralisation has been comparatively easy for well over a century, ever since the high Railway Age, it has been possible to develop a national, rather than a set of local, consciousnesses, except perhaps beyond the Highland Line. But this very property, which in hard times fosters conservatism, carries within itself the seeds of change. Centralism makes quick change easier, as the recent history of the curriculum and the promotion structure shows.

The educational future in Scotland will depend on the interaction of tradition with economic, social and political problems. They add up to alternative scenarios: the educational system is unlikely to be identical under minor devolution, federalism and independence. And there is another force to take into account, which I can only call the 'x' factor. It is the issue one does not foresee, but which is virtually certain to crop up. If this essay had been written in, say, 1960, it would not have mentioned two factors which have transformed Scottish society and so Scottish education—North Sea Oil and the Pill, both of which invaded the collective consciousness in the mid-sixties. The next 'x' factor may be some form of devolution not yet imagined; it may be an Economic Miracle; it may be something no one has even thought of.

The level of population is likely to remain remarkably steady until the end of the century. On present rates of emigration it should rise about one-half per cent; if the growth rate returns to those of the sixties the rise might be double that; if the decline in live births continues, there may even be an overall fall.[3] The geographical distribution is also likely to remain steady—two and a half millions in the west-central belt, one and a half in the east-central, a million north of that, a quarter of a million south. What is going to alter is the age-distribution. By the eighties one person in every six will be in retirement. On the other hand Table 1 illustrates some important trends affecting the number of young Scots at school:

Table 1: Present and Future (estimated) Pupil Population in Scotland

Educational Sector	1976-77 (thousands)	Session 1980-81 (thousands)	1984-85 (thousands)
Primary			
1973 Estimate	623	546.6	541.9
1976 Estimate	605.7	518.3	469.8
Secondary			
1973 Estimate	387	404.4	368
1976 Estimate	406	408.2	374.8
Total			
1973 Estimate	1,010	951	909.9
1976 Estimate	1,011.7	926.5	844.6

Both estimates emanated from the Scottish Education Department. The first observation to be made is that the total number of pupils is expected to fall in eight years by nearly 17 per cent. The decline will be worse in the primary sector (22.5 per cent) than the secondary (7.7 per cent), but the latter will be affected later. Since the Scottish system of recognising teachers' qualifications registers them separately for primary and secondary work, a shortage in the latter cannot be reduced by transferring surplus primary specialists—at least, not without retraining. Moreover, the comparison of estimates made only three years apart is instructive: it reflects a change in official thinking about two important factors. In 1973 the forecasters were still expecting the decline in the birth-rate to slow down; their successors still expect this, but at a markedly lower level. On the other hand, older pupils are staying on longer than expected: already a third of sixteen-year-olds and a fifth of seventeen-year-olds are in school, and the numbers in higher and further education have doubled in the last decade. In short, between now and the end of the century there will be an ageing population, with fewer primary and ultimately fewer secondary pupils, plenty of students in further education (espec-

ially if unemployment remains high), and a glut of teachers at all levels
while the output of large age-groups battles for places to teach the output of smaller ones.

The national economy, despite all the efforts to revive it, is unlikely
to show any spectacular transformation in the next decade or two. I
expect it to remain comparatively inflexible, with unemployment at far
too high a level. There will, of course, be many attempts at diversification:
none till now has been notably successful. Any that is achieved will have
to provide for extensive retraining of the work force, will also have to
cope with the problems generated by absentee landlords and senior
management, sure to be exacerbated by the need to attract external
capital. Oil remains the joker in the pack. Until the end of the century
it will buy time, creating jobs and some wealth but bringing many social
and political problems. Thereafter, the experts are agreed, the oil will
run out, and there had better be energy plans ready for the twenty-first
century.

All these trends will have a powerful influence on the educational
system. There will be the task of establishing a reasonably stable system
of job training and retraining within an unstable economy. Secondly,
there will be the call, not only to educate higher managers well, but to
convince incoming employers that they will get as good a job out of the
Scots as they would from their own. Thirdly, even when the oil starts
flowing freely, education is unlikely again to command the investment
it enjoyed in the sixties. As long as the current crisis lasts, indeed, the
problem will be to avoid the worst financial cuts; thereafter it will be to
establish a case for expansion. Everyone must pull in his belt these days,
but once it has been pulled there is a tendency to regard slackening as
unnecessary. Now education certainly has a good case for special treatment. The way out of the present troubles is to train experts, accomplished men and women at all levels and in all fields of work. To cut
down educational investment is to eat seed potatoes. But even a strong
argument like this would stand a better chance of convincing the Scotsman in the street if he felt the best use of educational funds had been
made so far. In the United Kingdom generally, and in Scotland at least
pro rata, education has had a fair crack of the whip. In the early sixties,
when the average percentage of gross domestic product assigned to educational work in twenty western countries was 3.6 per cent, the figure
in Britain was 4.8; in the early seventies it was 5.6 against a mean of
5.0, the nations ahead of us being Canada, the Netherlands, the United
States and the four Scandinavian states.[4] The verdict of a recent OECD
study is that education will find it increasingly hard in the next decade

to justify financial claims, and I agree with one Scottish Director, recently retired, when he writes:

> Education's share of the cake is as big as it is ever likely to be and bigger apparently than we can afford. I do not detect any widespread body of opinion that considers further expenditure on education justifiable.[5]

The political situation is likely to be determined for some time yet by the universal and imperative call by ordinary people for a louder voice in the decisions affecting their lives. This is the demand that calls for referenda, provides support for the Scottish National Party, brings militants in the trade unions out against the advice of their officials, and inspires general mistrust of authority, especially the 'faceless men' of Whitehall, St. Andrew's House and Regional Headquarters. Its manifestations are plain in education—councillors and committee members insisting on making decisions without the dictation (sometimes without the advice) of experts, students seeking representation on governing bodies, teachers demanding more places on national working parties and more say in running their own schools. The day, perhaps, is not far distant when a return may be made to the system in many nineteenth century burgh schools, where the headmaster was not a general but a kind of chairman of the board. Certainly he must nowadays accustom himself to the role of 'democratic leader' defined by Professor Castle,

> one who leads in co-operation, who prefers to inspire initiative in others rather than demonstrate his own . . . He will be a man who knows that he has not all the bright ideas and that the pooling of views not only contributes to the solution of problems, but ensures common obedience to decisions commonly agreed upon. His personal leadership will be evident only in the proved superiority of his contribution to the common task . . . The hall-marks of a democratic leader are intelligence, responsibility and humility.[6]

Of course, not everyone wants to be as active as this. Many parent-teacher associations owe their strength entirely to the headmaster and staff of the school. Tenants' associations, like so many groups, frequently depend on the energy of one man or woman. As for the new community councils one sometimes has the impression that they are answering demands people ought to be making, not those they are actually putting up. But some balance has to be found, and education will be expected to find it.

In the social background the most powerful factor is the present climate of egalitarianism, which has reached the point at which 'an equal chance for all' is not enough: there must be positive steps to equal- ise chances, to spend more time on the youngster who has had a bad start. Thus there is a new definition of the poverty level as the point at which a family is entitled to supplementary benefit. In schools the less articulate pupil claims a greater amount of the teacher's time, and this is the philosophy underlying the whole concept of guidance and counsel- ling. As with activism, not everyone is in agreement. At least one tenants' association in Glasgow, for instance, has demanded the power to veto applications for houses in its area, to prevent what it calls 'dumping' and the pioneers describe as 'a judicious social mix'. Very similar is the grow- ing call in the trade unions for the restoration and preservation of differ- entials. In our education we shall have to decide where we stand on this philosophy of equalisation.

These are some of the problems. What can education do about them in the next couple of decades? The idea that it can do anything at all is a matter of faith. I have already suggested that, in the current jargon, our investment has been rather less than cost-effective. We have the word of Her Majesty's Inspector of Constabulary that 'our society is less orderly than at any time during the past forty years',[7] on his statistics 14 per cent less than in 1972, 53 per cent less than in 1963. No one suggests that the increase is the *fault* of education, but there are plenty who claim that an effective educational programme would have produced more responsible attitudes in its pupils. A recent survey[8] names the favourite occupations of the Scottish people, in ascending order, as betting, bingo, dancing, watching football and looking at television. Employers frequently complain about how weak young job applicants are in spelling and arithmetic. Comprehensive education, which was expected by many of its supporters to break down class barriers, shows no evidence of having done so. On the other hand the statistics of the Scottish Certificate of Education show a steady, even spectacular increase in the number of presentations: over the period from 1970 to 1975 the figure at ordinary grade rose by 47.19 per cent and at higher by 20.26 per cent. Perform- ance, however, has not improved proportionately: the percentage increase over the same period at ordinary grade is 29.96, at higher 11.6, and higher passes have actually been falling since a peak of nearly 100,000 in 1973. Moreover, the examiners' reports frequently draw attention to the can- didates' weakness in written English.[9]

Cost-effective or not, education will be called upon to make a large contribution to the 'new Scotland', larger probably than it can hope to achieve—it has always been a convenient scapegoat in failure. Its first assignment, a very reasonable one, will be to develop appropriate work skills, in all fields, at all levels and with ample provision for retraining as conditions change. Its first problem will be to know exactly what is wanted At first sight employers and workers may be expected to know best: that is the principle on which the panels of SCOTEC[10] work, with their question naires, discussions, submissions, job profiles and proposals circulated for comment. But the principle operates on two presumptions—that there is a consensus in industry, and that industry really does know best. In fact, if decisions are left to employers and workers entirely, we must look for an emphasis on practice rather than theory, on how much more than why. This is certainly true, for instance, in teacher training: countless question-naires show students and teachers filling their ideal course with class man-agement and harping on 'relevance', by which they mean adaptation to immediate and obvious use. At its best such a programme reaches a level of specialisation which clarifies objectives and focusses resources. But it can be overdone, especially where retraining becomes necessary: we shall need a flexible system which 'does not close doors as they go along'.[11] These two principles, specialisation and flexibility, can be in opposition: we must strike an effective balance, which will not be achieved by training a man to be an electrician, however efficient, and nothing else.

There will be a special problem, in training for higher posts, a field in which Scotland has never excelled. A visible ladder of promotion is essential in creating the right psychological climate for work, but the problem of identification remains: a man does not prove he will be a good manager simply by being good at his job. Here also there are pro-bable tensions between specialists and generalists. The former distrusts general schemes, which, he thinks, trim the facts to fit the theory. The general planner is loath to leave everything to individual firms; by the nature of a capitalist economy, they are bound to be self-centred.

Academic bias may be weaker than it was, but traditional attitudes have by no means vanished, and are not likely to in the near future. In his novel *Roll of Honour* Eric Linklater wrote of a school staff 'from old Gilmour (the head) down to Patterson, who taught woodwork'. Technical education in Scotland has traditionally been low in the pecking order, and the other practical subjects, art and physical education, music and homecraft, have stood little higher. The results are obvious: any number of hard-working, shrewd teachers in these subjects, but rather few gen-uine highflyers; their work organised by directors and head masters who may have little interest and less experience in these fields; sometimes, notably in physical and domestic education, a propensity for clutching at respectability by packing the training with academic studies of marginal relevance. The Two Cultures in Scotland have been not so much arts and sciences as academic and practical studies, and a decade of schools-industry liaison has failed to destroy the barriers. Presuming that there will be a fair proportion of posts in higher management for Scots, they must evolve a better system for identifying and training them. They must also demolish the barriers between academic and practical studies: there is no place now for Voltaire's famous dictum that 'we have never claimed to educate chambermaids and stable boys: that is the portion of the angels'. This must be achieved, however, by raising the practical to the importance of the academic; the danger is that the academic may be forced down in value, as many believe it has already been.

The second task of Scottish education refers to the background factors, political, social and economic. For a growing number of Scots these have been emerging lately into the foreground: there may still be plenty of the *Lumpenproletariat* about, with no significant social or political interests, but recent events suggest a widespread, if vague and unformulated, desire at least to be consulted in these matters. This is a phenomenon educators must take into account: scholastic problems can never again be dealt with in isolation, as we may see from the recent history of comprehensive education and corporate management. Two recent educational statements illustrate this. Dr Nigel Grant asserted that 'those who are affected by decisions have a right and a duty to participate in taking them'. In a paper on *Education in the Seventies* the Aberdeen Junior Chamber of Commerce prophesies that people will work happily only if work, besides providing an opportunity to earn money, is intrinsically satisfying, like a craft, and holds out prospects of achievement, status and comradeship.[12]

The need for job satisfaction, of course, is fundamental; it always has been, but there has been little success in meeting it. One prescription is to help people develop their inner resources: schools have been trying to do *that* for many years, and it has proved to be a much more intricate job than they imagined. For instance, people ought to learn to make their own decisions, to accept responsibility. This will never be successful if the technique is simply throwing them in at the deep end, encouraging them to express their views on every subject under the sun without troubling to build those views on adequate evidence. The effect of this in the United States has been aptly described by Nabokov: 'Discussion in class, which means letting twenty young blockheads and two cocky neurotics discuss something with their teacher none of them knows anything about.' What we shall have to find in the next few years are better methods of helping Scottish pupils to express themselves while at the same time recognising when they have something worth expressing.

Moreover, exercising responsibility is hard work. No one wants to make decisions all the time; a good many, unfortunately, don't want to make them at all. Quite as strong as the desire for independence and the wish to be consulted, is the fundamental need for security. This displays itself everywhere, not least in the current vogue of nostalgia in entertainment. In education it is seen in a persistent hankering for traditional methods among employers, parents, pupils and teachers. The main reason for the existence of an independent school used to be to break free of the rigid state system; nowadays parents send their children to private schools in search of some rigour.

The existence of this demand for security is one of the main findings in two recent reports. Maciver and Fyfe,[13] investigating the factors affecting performance in ordinary grade examinations in Dundee, found that success correlated positively, not with socio-economic status, but with 'good attitudes' and stable human relationships. As for the recent Lancaster Survey which attracted so much attention in the popular press, what it demonstrated was not any essential superiority of traditional to experimental methods; but that any pursuit with a highly concentrated and clearly stated aim is likely to be quicker and more effective than one which is diffuse. It showed that pupils perform better when they know exactly what is required of them, traditional or experimental.

People, in short, want both responsibility and security, that is, not only the right to be consulted, but also the opportunity to switch off occasionally and rest in good hands. The danger in attempting to satisfy both demands is that education will fall between the two stools, and recent Scottish efforts have done precisely that. Pupils now speak up for themselves more than they did, but have not been convinced that opinions ought to be based on solid evidence. Furthermore, no atmosphere of mutual trust has been fostered between pupils and teachers, teachers and parents, teachers and administrators, amateurs and professionals. Such trust was no doubt exploited sometimes in the past; authority was abused. But in recent years the pendulum has swung too far. This atmosphere of trust must be re-established in Scottish schools and universities, and our education, though it cannot do this alone, will shoulder most of the task.

Ask the Scotsman in the street, that elusive character, what schools ought to be teaching in the next decade, and it is a good bet that the first thing he will ask for is conscientiousness, what he calls 'a fair day's work for a fair day's pay'. There is a widespread conviction abroad that 'they', however he defines them, are not working hard or devotedly enough, and that is why we are in our present difficulties, buying foreign cars, for example, because they are thought to be more reliable. We are paying now for the decline of the dogma, that work is a virtue in itself. Even if Scotsmen paid it only lip-service, it was always there; stating that nothing of any value in the world was to be gained without working for it, and that in any case labour was good for the character. Nowadays there is no agreed ethic, and some resentment at anybody who offers one, as the General Teaching Council discovered when they sought to establish a Code of Practice for Scottish teachers. One of the things education will be expected to provide in the next twenty years, indeed as soon as possible, is an ethic to promote conscientiousness, the will to work, a selfless contribution to the good of the community. As with everything else, it cannot do this alone. Society must decide whether it genuinely believes in cooperation and mutual trust, and for that matter whether it believes in original sin, or simply that, if we can only get the environment right, then everyone will join the angels.

How likely is Scottish education to achieve all its aims, or even to make some progress, during the rest of this century? Only an incurable optimist—or of course pessimist—would expect a radical change, unless the 'x' factor turns out to be a visit from the Archangel Gabriel. For the first part of this period, five years at least, education will be busy enough merely surviving in the economic typhoon. The battles will be over retrenchment: new ideas are unlikely to command support unless they promote financial savings, and that probably entails a shift towards authoritarianism. Partly for these economic reasons, and partly from the prevailing spirit of pragmatism, educators are likely to concentrate much more of their attention on practical objectives like developing specific work skills, and much less on more general aims in the social and political fields. All this will come at a time when Scotland's political future will be unsettled. The more independence is achieved, the further left the government is likely to move, and the better disposed it will be to liberal experiment; on the other hand, while economic hardship persists, the proverbial hard-headedness of the Scot will probably push towards élitism. The less independent the future state, the stronger the bonds the devolutionary system retains with the United Kingdom, the longer the political battles will rage, and the less time there will be for purely educational debates.

The comprehensive system will continue. Whatever happens in places like Tameside, however unhappy some parents may be, the consequences

of the government's decision are now irreversible, and in many schools
the system is working well. It is essential that the system caters gener-
ously for its minorities, for people whose religious, social or educational
conscience will not allow them to rest content in a comprehensive system. Ideally the government ought to make arrangements for them inside the system, but if it cannot or will not, then they must be provided
for outside it. I expect a left-wing government to do its best to discourage
such dissent; I would be extremely unhappy if it forbade it altogether. It
will be a sad day for democracy when the minorities are bullied out of
existence.

Within the comprehensive structure there may well be a swing back
from the more extreme forms of egalitarianism. If we want efficiency,
we really must stop being so mealy-mouthed, even for the best-hearted
of reasons, about individual performance. But it is the next step that will
count in the immediate future—what is done for the 'less well endowed'.
It may not be possible to afford compensatory education for them;
already, in the economic crisis, one of the liveliest complaints of the
left is that the pupils likeliest to suffer from cuts are those in under-
privileged areas. If funds become more plentiful, the debate will be on
whether the calls of national efficiency will force us back into streaming. In a hard time—and the next twenty years will certainly be that—it
is common sense to use all our natural advantages, and one of the most
powerful of these resides in our clever children. They have had less than
their fair share of attention recently, and it is not enough to suggest that
they will contrive anyway to survive. I should be surprised if the concept of streaming, in its traditional form, were reintroduced. On the
other hand, I shall be equally surprised if the traditional realism of the
Scot does not assert itself, and cause more attention to be paid to the
'more well endowed'. It will probably be accomplished by fiddling around
with notions like 'setting'. It would be pleasant to think that it would be
achieved by a return to intellectual honesty, with people no longer
being exercised when anyone gets anything everyone else does not get.
But that I do not expect. It will come more quickly under devolution,
more slowly with independence. If there is any durability in 'Scottish
educational traditions', it *will* come; the pendulum is due to swing.

Notes

1. Scotland, J., *The History of Scottish Education*, (ULP, 1969), vol. 2, pp. 255-76.

2. Mann, *Report for 1843*, p. 381.

3. Scottish Information Office, *Scotland at Your Fingertips*, HMSO 1975; Murray, G.T., *Scotland: the New Future*, (Blackie, 1973), pp. 6-10.

4. OECD Studies in Resource Allocation, *Public Expenditure on Education July 1976*, HMSO 1976.

5. Alex McLellan, in GTC News Letter No. 9, October 1976.

6. Castle, E.B., *Ancient Education and Today*, (Penguin, 1961), p. 203.

7. HMIC for Scotland, Report for 1974, pp. 44-7.

8. Murray, op.cit., pp. 218-19.

9. Scottish Certificate of Education Examinations Board, *Report for 1975*, HMSO 1976, 12, pp. 79-80, my percentages.

10. Scottish Technical Education Council.

11. Grant, N. in *The Red Paper on Scotland* EUSPB 1975, p. 363.

12. Grant, op. cit., pp. 358-9; Aberdeen Junior Chamber of Commerce, Entry for the Urwick Orr Award (1974), p. 2.

13. Maciver, L. and Fyfe, T.W., *A Study of Non-Intellectual Factors affecting O-grade Performance*, Dundee College of Education (1975).

8 TRENDS IN THE ECONOMY

Andrew Hargrave

The framework to economic activity comprises natural resources, human and material. The way we assess them, organise them, develop them, exploit them, are in themselves the signposts to the future. Development —or the lack of it—takes place in an increasingly interdependent world. The possession of certain natural resources does not by itself guarantee success: these have to relate to human wants.

Scotland, whether a region of the UK, a devolved area with a legislative Assembly but subordinate to the Westminster Parliament, a federal state sharing power with Westminster, or a self-governing nation, will remain geographically in the British Isles, and part of Europe. She is also within the European and Atlantic communities politically; economically by far the largest proportion of her trade is with other parts of the UK. These are factors which would remain unaffected by constitutional change, certainly in the short term, politically and economically. On the other hand, constitutional change might well foster the self-reliance whose existence is essential for any community wishing to grow and advance.

The use of manpower is a significant factor, perhaps more so than any other, in success or failure in the economic sphere. One way of quantifying progress in the use of manpower is in the field of education and training: the numbers attaining certain levels of qualifications or participating in training leading to professional or manual skills. In 1966, 68 per.cent of Scottish school leavers left without a certificate of any kind, Ordinary or Higher grade. By 1974 (the last year for which detailed figures were available at the time of writing) the proportion had declined to 42 per cent. Moreover, one boy or girl in five left school with three 'Highers' or more, the normally accepted minimum for university entrance. In the same year, around 200,000 students received higher education of one kind or another, including a proportion of non-Scots: but then a number of Scots were studying outside Scotland possibly compensating for this.

Unfortunately, many of these highly trained and qualified Scots were and still are leaving Scotland, partly because the 'branch plant'[1] economy is unable to absorb the products of universities and colleges of higher education. There are insufficient jobs in terms of quality, prospects and remuneration. As the 1971 Census of Production indicated in relation to administrative employment, Scotland had 2.6 per cent of managerial and 3.8 per cent of professional posts. This compared with an average for Great Britain of 3.6 per cent and 4.7 per cent respectively. The share of South-East England, nerve centre of the over-centralised UK, was 4.8 per cent and 6.1 per cent.

Over-centralisation is underlined by a glance at the 'Times 1,000 Companies'.[2] Of these only 4.7 per cent had their registered offices in Scotland: 53.2 per cent—more than half—had their offices in London. The same applies to research and development establishments. A study[3] has shown that in 1970 Scotland had 7.3 per cent of such establishments compared with 49.2 per cent being located in the South-East of England. The Scottish proportion would have been even lower had it not been for some Government institutes, mainly in the agricultural and marine fields which are closely related to the domestic economy. In the private sector, Scotland had only 5.4 per cent of the industrial research establishments, 2.9 per cent of other private research and 2.2 per cent of the research associations. The comparative figures for South-East England were 45.2 per cent, 77.4 per cent and 44.4 per cent respectively. It has been over-centralisation on such a scale, evident in all spheres of administration and development, public as well as private, which has deprived Scotland of her highly trained, able and enterprising people. It is this that has led to a general lowering of talent, entrepreneurial and leadership and, indirectly, to the 'begging bowl' mentality.

The trend must be reversed for the quality of economic activity—indeed of life itself—to be improved in the long term. It cannot, however, be reversed without conscious political, social and administrative action which might include: discrimination in favour of enterprise with a large element of 'creative' function—managerial decision-making, research, development, marketing. Encouragement and promotion might be by way of the traditional means in the short term—tax concessions, grants, loans, advisory and infrastructural aid, the provision of physical facilities. In the longer term, such encouragement might include deliberate expansion and promotion of domestically generated, owned and financed enterprise, an organic and planned link between enterprise and the relevant educational and training institutions and bodies. Constitutional change would not by itself bring about such action: but its extent and success would clearly depend on Scots being in a position to make the necessary decisions. So the next few years may well set the pattern for decades in the use of manpower at all levels, including technical and manual skills.

In 1974, almost 54 per cent of the boys leaving school in Scotland entered apprenticeship,[4] a higher proportion than in any other area in the UK and fully 13 per cent more than in 1971. At the same time, more than one-third of boys and girls left school without any formal training whatever which compares unfavourably with other advanced industrial nations. Yet, if Scotland's industrial effort is to be upgraded, as it should be, so has the quality of the people who sustain it. It is a continuing process which starts with young people entering a University, technical or commercial college or apprenticeship and goes on until the end of their working lives.

Ten years ago, one expert[5] went so far as to say that

in future the training given to a worker under 21 will be largely out of date by the time he is 31; when he is 40 he may well need to be trained again and a whole series of additional training periods will be required to enable him to cope with situations, machines and processes unthought of when he was an apprentice.

Since then, obsolescence of machines and processes has accelerated further, and the industrialisation of a large part of what is generally called the Third World has taken place. Its direct effect was acutely felt in Scotland recently when Govan Shipbuilders lost a large cargo ship contract to Hyundal Shipbuilders of South Korea. The expansion of various industries now takes place elsewhere, the motor industry largely in Latin America, Brazil and Mexico in particular: consumer electronics in Hong Kong, Singapore, Taiwan and South Korea; refinery and petro-chemical development in the Middle East, Venezuela, Iran and other oil-producing states.

The 'branch-plant' economy and its effect on opportunities in Scotland has already been mentioned: but it now seems as if the traditional sources for branch-plants, the US and other multinationals, are looking elsewhere for investment locations. (This is born out by recent statistics on investment enquiries.)[6] Upgrading for Scottish industry and its work force is therefore essential for both reasons; the accelerating pace of change in situations, machines and processes as well as the growing competition in the relatively less sophisticated production and assembly operations. To some extent, adult training and re-training programmes in Scotland have responded to this challenge, no doubt reinforced by the easier availability of trainees through unemployment. The expansion of such programmes between 1975 and the early months of 1976 is illustrated by Table 1:

Table 1: Training Opportunities for Adults—1970-75, Scotland and Great Britain

	1970	1971	1972	1973	1974	1975+
Skill centres	1,666	1,484	1,976	1,996	1,877	1,846
Colleges of Further Education	108	210	816	2,615	3,647	4,930
Employers' premises	7	44	851	1,089	711	718
Total	1,781	1,738	3,543	5,700	6,235	7,494
% of women	2.3	6.0	13.1	32.5	51	55 (Est.)
% of GB total	10.7	11.2	12.2	14.2	13.5	11.5 (Est.)

+ Provisional

Special measures for young people:	Aug.-Dec. 1975 completions 250
Training within industry — total trained:	1974 3,440 (20% of GB)
	1975 4,342 (% NA)
Award Schemes:	
Shipbuilding	264 apprentice applications approved,
Engineering, etc.	385 under training, 363 more available
Premium Grants Scheme for Apprentices	760 (plus 20 non-craft) so far

Source: Training Services Agency (TSA).

Impressive as such progress may appear only the surface of the problem has been touched. The number of adults affected is still below one per cent of the total Scottish labour force compared with Sweden's two to three per cent at any time.

Naturally, people detached from their workplaces for training, whether managers, technologists, technicians, commercial staff or craftsmen, are temporarily outside the productive process for the company which employs them as well as for the economy as a whole. But they are in the same category as capital investment, saved from profits or borrowed and withdrawn from immediate consumption in the form of dividends for shareholders or lower taxes for the taxpayers. Ultimately, the return on such investment must be a gain in efficiency, viability, profitability and in the changes to survive. In any case, if one of the main objectives to achieve improved economic performance is self-reliance of those who sustain it, it can certainly be better served by people who are better trained as well as flexible in their attitudes throughout their working lives. If Scotland is to avoid stagnation and decay in the longer term, training programmes will have to be substantially expanded, their contents more

closely related to the process of upgrading scientific and technical requirements which should itself be more closely related to conditions prevailing throughout the world. These programmes should be reviewed at frequent intervals and the participants safeguarded against loss of promotion
and pay prospects.

However, in one field, the Scottish decision-maker may already find
a domestic outlet. Many financial institutions, while overshadowed by
the City of London, have nevertheless succeeded in retaining their identity
and playing a not inconsiderable part in financing such massive operations as North Sea oil and gas exploration and development. The Bank
of Scotland, for example, is a founder member (with a 15 per cent stake)
in the International Energy Bank, leader of the consortium financing the
Piper and Claymore fields. The Royal Bank of Scotland has provided finance for a good deal of the on- and off-shore supplies and services and
the Clydesdale Bank (although a wholly owned subsidiary of the Midland
Bank)[7] for the platform builders. North Sea Assets, the largest investment
company for supplies and services, has the merchant bank Noble Grossart
as its founder and operational manager.

Scotland's nine life insurance offices include Standard Life, the UK's
largest, and also one of the largest pension fund managers, and a further
three are among the top half dozen. General Accident is among the top
four or five 'composite' insurance companies. The top five UK finance
houses providing hire-purchase and leasing finance include Lloyd's &
Scottish in which the Royal Bank has a 41 per cent stake. About one-
third of all UK investment trust funds are controlled by institutions located in Scotland. The Scottish institutions have to compete on an international scale, not only with their big rivals in London, New York, Frank-
furt, Zurich, Amsterdam and Tokyo, but also with the branch offices set
up in Scotland in recent years, including five by US and two by French
institutions. The National Westminster Bank, the only London clearing
bank without a direct stake in Scottish banking now has branches in
Edinburgh and Glasgow: a further branch in Aberdeen is also in prospect.
The influx into Scotland of these and other Banks (including branches
of prominent merchant banks), finance houses and other institutions is
to some extent a recognition of Scotland's significance as a financial
centre. In another sense, however, it also underlines Scotland's 'branch
plant' economy.

One important reason for the non-Scottish institutions branching into
Scotland is to provide a service to industrial and commercial companies
whose headquarters are in London, in New York, in Paris, in Toronto or
Montreal—in other words, the incomers who now provide the greater

proportion of manufacturing employment in Scotland. It is in part an explanation for the relatively low proportion of Scottish bank advances going into manufacturing industry (Table 2).

Table 2: Composition of Lending by Scottish and London Clearing Banks 1971-4 (November figures in percentages)

	LONDON %			SCOTTISH %		
	1971	1973	1974	1971	1973	1974
Manufacturing	26.5	33.5	37.6	34.2	26.6	32.4
Other production*	15.1	14.6	14.4	19.2	14.1	15.7
Personal	18.0	21.0	17.1	12.0	15.6	13.4
Services	21.8	18.7	18.5	25.8	24.8	22.6
Property	4.2	6.5	6.0	2.8 ⎫	5.1 ⎫	4.4 ⎫
Other financial	4.4	5.7	6.4	6.0 ⎭ 8.8	13.8 ⎭ 18.9	11.5 ⎭ 15.9

Source: Wood, Mackenzie & Co.
* agriculture, fishing, forestry, mining, construction.

A further reason may be Government aid to industry in the form of development grants, selective loans, interest relief, training and removal grants as well as the Regional Employment Premium which indirectly frees funds for investment (Table 3).

Table 3: Advances Outstanding by Scottish Clearing Banks on 20 August 1975

	Total (£m)	% of advances
Manufacturing	423.9	22.0
Other production	316.0	16.8
Personal	248.8	13.3
Services	429.5	26.3
Financial (incl. property)	242.5	12.9
Overseas residents	151.3	8.9
	1,875.0	100.0

Source: Association of Scottish Clearing Banks.

Any reversal in the trend towards further 'multinationalisation' of Scottish industry would, of course, be reflected in the transaction structures as well as financial policies of Scottish institutions. They have, after all, played a prominent role in the expansion of trade in Scotland in the eighteenth century and in the industrial revolution of the nineteenth. Their response to the North Sea challenge could be a portent to reaction to a similar challenge in other areas of industry, trade and commerce.

North Sea oil and gas exploration has brought about substantial changes in the infrastructure of Scotland. Roads had to be improved and new ones built to platform sites, ports and pipeline terminals. Ports themselves have had to be dredged and expanded. Houses and schools have had to be provided for oil-related workers and their families. As the production phase gains momentum there is bound to be a gradual decline in exploration activity. While the present comparative lull in rig activity and the dearth of orders for production platforms may only be temporary, the peak in terms of exploration and preparation for production may well have been passed. This in turn has profound implications for some of the areas which benefited most from oil-related work, such as the North-East coast and the Cromarty Firth. Isolated spots such as Methil, in Fife, where the Redpath Dorman-Long (BSC) platform yard has run out of work and is threatened with closure are a warning to what might happen to Aberdeen or the small towns clustered around the Cromarty Firth. Shetland faces less of a problem as most of its construction labour is an immigrant one: Sullom Voe, expected to be the largest oil port in Europe, will on the other hand have a sizable permanent staff.

If the quality and content of Scottish industry is to be upgraded, rehabilitation of the environment will have to go a good deal further than the £120 million Glasgow East End project which is only one of the several eyesores as well as heartaches in industrial Scotland. The desired upgrading of Scottish industry assumes that heavy industry such as platform construction and other, largely semi-skilled and unskilled labour intensive ones will give way to more sophisticated manufacturing operations requiring less bulky but more speedy forms of transport, within Scotland, to other parts of the UK and overseas. Fortunately, many of the facilities for change already exist. Scotland's east coast ports, from Grangemouth and Leith to Peterhead, have been improved and expanded to cope with supply traffic to exploration rigs; Prestwick Airport, one of Britain's leading air trade outlets to North America, has a great deal of spare capacity; road and rail access to the ports and airports have also been improved to cope with North Sea related traffic.

A question mark hangs over the future workload pattern of Clydeport which is currently still the largest Scottish port for both oil and non-oil cargoes. In 1975, oil traffic alone fell by about a third or 4.2

million tons. It was the result of general decline in oil imports due to the recession as well as to the escalating price of imported crude oil. But, with North Sea oil gradually replacing perhaps as much as two-thirds of imported crude, overseas oil traffic to BP's Finnart terminal which handles the bulk of Clydeport's oil is to contract further. It will be replaced as the Clyde's main bulk cargo by iron ore to be handled at the British Steel Corporation's new terminal at Hunterston. The terminal will have a capacity of eight to ten million tons of ore and is likely to be under-utilised for many years yet. On the other hand, the facility could be made available for other types of bulk cargo.

Clydeport's general cargo traffic has also suffered in recent years, partly through competition from other UK ports which has among others kept the container port under-utilised and partly through the continuing economic decline of the West of Scotland. Yet the deep-water end of the port at Hunterston still represents one of the greatest potential natural harbours in Europe: the problem is how to sell it to shippers; how to establish more efficient links with continental Europe, possibly as a transit for East coast ports, as in the original Oceanspan idea:[8] and how to develop it as a trading post between Europe and the fast-growing industrial areas of the world, including the Far East and Latin America.

Many parts of Scotland have undergone major changes in the first half of the 1970's as a result of the North Sea boom, of which the big holes at Ardyne Point, Nigg and Loch Kishorn are only a few outstanding examples. Though of less magnitude than the industrial revolution of the nineteenth century in terms of devastated countryside, polluted air and water, a major task of rehabilitation and restoration of the ecological balance lies ahead. Employment is only one aspect of the problem: like the seeding of ancient coal bings in areas of dead pits, rehabilitation concerns aesthetics and recreation as well. Infrastructure planning is part of an integrated process of overall planning for the future— for the economy, for education and training, even for food production and forestry. All these entail a degree of control over resources and their allocation. The constitutional options have major relevance to the future economic framework of Scotland.

Whatever the priorities laid down by parliamentary and economic agencies and institutions, private effort and initiative and public consent, the sign-posts should always carry two directions: one pointing to the domestic situation and a second one encompassing the world. This should ensure that the urgent need for rehabilitation at home—bad housing, urban depravation, social evil, gaps in education and training, structural reform in industry—does not overshadow and blank out the world outside, the greater part of which requires rehabilitation on a much grander scale: and, on the other hand, gazing at the broader horizons does not deflect attention from the need at home. Such 'two-horizon thinking' should enable Scots to contemplate the last quarter of the twentieth century in dynamic terms, using the past as a springboard for future action rather than as a source of sterile reminiscing, irrelevant traditions and pride.

Notes

1. J.R. Firn: 'Location of ultimate ownership of Scottish manufacturing plant and employment 1973', in a series of *Scotsman* articles 31 October to 2 November 1973. He shows that only 41.2 per cent of total manufacturing employment is controlled by Scottish firms; 39.8 per cent is controlled by English, 14.9 per cent by North American and the rest by other non-Scottish firms.

2. Westaway, J., 'Times 1,000 companies' quoted in *Regional Studies* March 1974.

3. Buswell, R.S. and Lewis, E.W.: 'The Geographical Distribution of Industrial Research Activity in the UK', *Regional Studies*, vol. 4, no. 3, 1970.

4. Department of Employment Gazette, December 1975.

5. W.D. Seymour: 'Retraining for Technical Change', *IPM Journal*, December 1966.

6. *Scottish Economic Bulletin*, nos. 9-10: Winter 1975-Summer 1976.

7. Barclays Bank has a 35 per cent holding in the Bank of Scotland; Lloyds a 16.5 per cent share in the Royal Bank's equity.

8. *Oceanspan Reports*, nos. 1 and 11, published by the Scottish Council (Development and Industry, February 1970 and October 1971).

9 THE OUTLOOK FOR INDUSTRY

John Evans

It is difficult for one to dissociate economic from political developments in Scotland, particularly if one is both Scottish and deeply involved in industrial development. At the time of writing, the Scotland and Wales Bill is wending its way through Committee. It seems apparent that, unless there is a change in UK government, it will slip through without significant amendment. The result will be, I feel, to re-establish Scotland on the very slippery slope that the publication of the 1975 White Paper temporarily averted: for there is a very curious dynamic in the Scottish political world. In my view this *Schluss* leads to no turning area—no ability, even to slalom—and can only terminate at *Ziel*, where the federalised powers will be few. Should there be a change in the tone of the UK government, there would certainly emerge a major power group dedicated to the maintenance of the Union. It could be that for some time separatist pressures would be subdued; but I cannot foresee this as being in any way a stable position.

When, or if, independence is obtained, the situation would still be unstable. An upheaval of proportions unprecedented since the major switch of the industrial base during the Second World War must occur. The characteristics of such an upheaval would be dictated by both indigenous and foreign elements. Subjective prejudice suggests that within the next two decades virtual autonomy over certain powers, mainly economic, is inevitable. It is an area wracked by jargon; but, recently, I learned what the phrase 'the greatest concentration of multiple urban deprivation in Western Europe' meant. It meant that in Glasgow housing is hellish, job prospects are poorer. My informant pointed out that Dundee might soon take over the mantle. Westminster policy-makers, who do, after all, operate within a UK framework, have done little to ameliorate this decline since the war. Despite massive injections of new capital and aid to industry, the consensus view appears to feel central government policy to be too unaware of the nature of the industrial and commercial environment which it tries to deal with, and with the aspirations of its electorate. In this environment, one cannot see either the devolutionist position of the British Labour Party, or the *status quo ante* with segments of the Conservative Party succeeding. 'Independence is about jobs' is the cry: those with jobs, or without, their spouses and

119

their offspring, are the voters.

Myths and legends explaining Scotland's relative industrial decline abound. The most commonly held view is that of *outdatedness*—that is, that the various locational factors, which determine the optimal location in Scotland of plants in certain industries, have now been eroded. These are variously listed: the grit, pluck and craftsmanship of the Clydesider is known the world over; similarly, all know about the foundation of the Scottish heavy engineering industry on iron ore, coal or shale oil. For fifty, or a hundred years, the basic manufacturing operations have continued despite the exhaustion of these justifications. The major logical defences of this situation are antiacademic and pragmatic. Location theory might be all right on the homogeneous German plain; theories of industrial linkage, multipliers, import substitution, and so on, are excellent until applied to reality. Industrial location is determined by many factors, mostly immeasurable: what is the time rate of discount on investment that the Board requires; what is the minimum life of the project in relation to that; where does the Managing Director's wife want to live; what is some consultant's expectation of the development of various kindred technologies, or skills, in the area?

In a very large economy, such as that of the USA, undoubtedly generalised theories can be demonstrated to fall within the bounds of statistical significance. Within the EEC, owing to the preponderance of a multitude of local pressures, this will not foreseeably be the case. In Scotland, it is absurd to use such 'laws' in examining the likely development of the industrial structure. The country is too small, the decisions too subjective: the easy option for policy-makers, to particularise from generalities, is untenable. Industry is a very local phenomenon. Consider an economy like that of Austria. Although the hard 'base' is largely determined by the welfare of a handful of a few large firms, the bulk of manufacturing employment is located in small workshops and factories, whose very existence would be in severe doubt if location theory had any practical basis. In London and Glasgow, a huge amount of industry has persisted in areas which have no perceptible locational advantage. Sociologists have invoked significant reasons for their prevalence: but that defies academic logic. The inheritance of land, labour or capital provides a very strong counterweight to industrial mobility. However, the industries and locations discussed so far are examples of *historical* and continuing location. In Scotland the discussion revolves around newly discovered natural resources—land, labour and capital—and a completely new opportunity to rebuild an industrial base. (May I emphasise that a stable industrial base is not essential to the systematic progression

of an economy. Stability is not apparent in the Republic of South
Africa, which is one of the fastest growing industrial economies in the
world; nor of the Cayman Islands, which have one of the highest rates
of growth of *per capita* income.)

The *Scotsman* recently reported a new national record in the numbers
of unemployed. It gained the page one lead position. For some months,
there had been a UK-wide dispute amongst civil servants in the Department of Employment over the collation of such statistics. Senior civil
servants had underestimated the slope of the unfortunate trend. The
casual observer who reads his paper faithfully should not have been
greatly surprised, for the ingredients to the mess were apparent, and
written about all the time. The redundancies and factory closures were
well publicised; the data on still unemployed school-leavers were released
earlier by Social Work departments. Factory closures and redundancies
lead to the operation of the multiplier—or 'divider'—mentioned above.
When local base industry's real output declines, so must real incomes,
but by some multiplier of the original decline. That is, in a country as
small as Scotland, there must be a few key industries or firms, on which
the welfare of the community depends. (Nationalists argue that this is
the essence of the point that the bulk of the Commons fails to appreciate:
England, they feel, has far greater horizontal integration.)

Consider the Inverness area. The traditional staple industry is in the
primary sector: agriculture, forestry and some fishing. Tourism is a
major source of total activity (but a recent study for the Highlands and
Islands Development Board shows that in return for that activity pretty
little local value added is achieved). The non-primary income in the area
revolves around a very few activities. There is an outburst of contractors
and depots at Muir-of-Ord; small industries clustering around the coast;
and then the giants. MK-Shand at Saltness, British Aluminium's glossy
smelter at Invergordon; and Brown & Root-Wimpey at Nigg Point; A. I.
Welders in Inverness, and McDermott's fabrication yard at Ardesier.
From thence, the hinterland. The closure of any one of these plants
would be catastrophic for the district, but Government, whether in Westminster or, as presently constituted, in Edinburgh, seems to view life
very much in terms of *trends*: 'An upturn is anticipated in steel platform
orders following the licensing of new blocks', 'the forecast upturn in
the demand for private domestic dwellings will . . . '. This is not the
case. Activity in Easter Ross and Inverness depends critically on the com-
petitiveness of the tenders submitted by the plants.

Again, consider Chrysler at Paisley. The UK government has, no
doubt, some long term strategy over the assembly of motor vehicles. The

retention of Linwood, with massive government support was negotiated with one side not knowing the objectives of the other. The decision over the future of that plant lay outside the terms of the debate; instead of UK production capacity, the *numeraires* in the dispute were those of the world demand for cars of a particular sort, of Chrysler's own forecast role in that, and of the relative effectiveness of their different plants in manufacturing the product. UK demand was of no relevance: multinational strategy was, and although one hopes not, possibly the gullibility of governments. It would be tedious to draw out the debate in an attempt to demonstrate that the macro-economic analysis of micro-industry is a farcical exercise when one is concerned with an economy as small as Scotland's. The events on the ground are those that will determine future performance.

A further red herring is that of the ownership of Scottish industry in the future. No doubt, under a regime of substantial devolution, or even independence, there would be very serious problems over the taxation—or subsidisation—of a significant proportion of industry—they are problems for legislators to examine and attempt to solve. The aspect of the problem considered in this speculative essay is the relationship between ownership and control, and again between those factors and the structure of linkages with the rest of the economy. Ownership, in de-institutionalised terms, means little. Chrysler, perhaps, benefit from Detroit masters and the long term viability of Chrysler worldwide depends on them. Linwood may, in the short term, suffer. IBM, on the other hand, are unlikely ever to reduce the level of activity in their Spango Valley (Greenock) plant in any way disproportionate to the activity level of IBM worldwide.

On the other hand, some plants in Scotland owned by multi-nationals operate with almost complete autonomy. A large mechanical engineering plant in the Grampian region operates under the banner of a huge American conglomerate: but its only contact with it, apart from medium-term financial accountability, is in using it as a 'preferred' sub-contractor. There is certainly an acceleration towards the 'devolution' of plant management; and it has little to do with the parentage of the plants. While movements on the political front may be one factor, it is doubtful whether it is a particularly significant one. (Unlike, for example, the headlong rush to Edinburgh of English and overseas financial institutions, which appears to be determined by political judgement.) The devolution of industrial control appears to be largely due to an evolving change in the prevalent theories of management stratagems.

Industrial change will be overwhelmingly dominated by two groups of factors: firstly, the industrial strategy of officialdom, and, secondly, the faith that industry is prepared to put on that strategy. Consider, first, the strategies that might emerge under the three political regimes discussed earlier. The *status quo ante*, it was suggested, could only prevail under the conditions of a major swing to the right at Westminster. One would assume that this would lead to a decline in interventionist policies in relation to industry—although political sensitiveness would presumably force the preservation of the industrial powers of the Scottish Development Agency. Industrial development policies might follow the pattern of the Macmillan era, when such plants as Chrysler and the pulp and paper mill at Corpach were directed to their particular locations. A further feature might be the farming out of projects on a UK-wide basis, a logic that is coherent only in political terms. (An example often cited is the British Steel Corporation's plan for a major plant development: under political pressure it was arbitrarily divided between Llanwern and Ravenscraig. The allocation of new aluminium smelters in the 1960s is also interesting because not only were the three smelters spread over three regions but over three operating companies.)

It was suggested that the political backdrop to such an industrial policy was one of instability. The uncertainty induced would probably discourage industrialists from certain types of investment. Self-contained units, manufacturing finished products with a high degree of vertical integration, might well be unaffected. On the other hand, the development of plants involved in the partial processing of materials or the manufacture of components for integration into a final product elsewhere might be inhibited. An example of an 'island' site might be the steel fabrication yard at Ardesier; an example of the latter could be any of the recently established electronic components plants in the central belt whose products are integrated into finished goods elsewhere. Certainly, whatever major new projects are encouraged by central government will be encouraged with UK interests in mind. The activities of the SDA would be likely to be circumscribed to some extent: but should it remain autonomous, the fight would be something of a mismatch. In UK terms, where does the Scottish economy relatively stand? The predominant factors could only operate to Scotland's short term benefit. The first is the very serious unemployment level, higher than any part of the UK other than Northern Ireland. In UK political terms, ignoring any other variables, that is quite unacceptable and must lead to regional development policies of the Macmillan type mentioned above— large development policies which generate little industrial activity outside the plants themselves. Their major virtue is that of sponging up local pockets of unemployment.

The other major factor that would lead to a net short-term gain is that of off-shore petroleum. It is in the UK interest to develop all commercial fields in the shortest possible time. Significant employment will be generated by such a policy, and, through the growth of Scottish oil-related industries and expertise, there will be considerable secondary and tertiary employment and income generation as well. The base of this activity is, of course, unstable—as recent redundancies at Bredero Price and MK-Shand (both pipe-coaters) and the platform yards at Nigg, Methil and Ardyne Point show. The social and environmental effects of the volatility in levels of activity are considerable. Spin-off from the industry generated to serve off-shore developments do produce economic benefits of a longer-term nature. The expertise that is growing is leading to increased involvement in the oil industry elsewhere, both in unspectacular areas such as the manufacture of specialist pumps, or non-slip gratings for rigs and platforms, or in massive contracts such as that won by McDermott's for a £20 million platform jacket for Brazil. Experience in *technologies* rather than products might also produce benefits: the MacAlpine Sea Tank platform yard at Ardyne Point is marketing large concrete rafts of cellular structure. However, such longer-term developments might take place under any political regime.

Downstream activities—the processing of the crude oil and natural gas—would also be subject to a strong locational pull towards Scotland. Where the petroleum is landed by pipeline there are strong commercial advantages in breaking it up into a number of constituent parts near the landing terminal. The plants, which are of considerable size, can employ several hundred people. Further processing of the fractions would probably be done elsewhere in existing petrochemical complexes (the exception to this is the refinery at Grangemouth, which was built before the war but has been subject to massive recent expansion). When North Sea petroleum dries up, the new refineries and treatment plants will suffer from severe locational disadvantages. It is difficult to predict a more satisfactory future for them than for the concrete production platform yards—although their viability can be measured in terms of a generation rather than the six or seven years that currently seem viable for the platform builders.

Under the existing proposals for a Scottish Assembly, the general picture should be similar to that just described. The SDA is responsible to the Secretary of State, rather than to the Assembly; the Assembly is given no industrial powers. On the assumption that the proposals pass through Parliament and do lead to a stable situation, the only difference in pattern that can be foreseen is a hiatus in industrial development while industrialists attempt to assess the nature and permanence of the stability.

The third political prospect is that of independence, or at least of the devolution of very substantial economic powers—those of fiscal policy (including subsidies), perhaps monetary policy, and powers over the control of industry. There is no reason to suppose that a satisfactory fiscal package cannot be worked out, and implemented over a short period of time. There would be a period of uncertainty which might deter some companies from expanding their activities in Scotland, but it is difficult to see that any plants would actually be closed in that period. An economically powerful Edinburgh administration would be forced to continue within the pre-existing framework in its relationship with industry: a situation dictated both by practicality and by Brussels. There is, however, a great deal less certainty over the transfer of monetary policy. The Scottish National Party argue that a smooth transition to a Scottish Central Bank would take a year; they are ignoring the complexities of the financial system and the chameleon-like nature of many financial institutions. The impact on industry of a long drawn out transition is uncertain. Large companies make financial transactions on a world, rather than a national, scale anyway. Small companies will get damaged in the confusion unless special arrangements are made to protect their interests.

Scottish control over industry, however, would seem to generate few transitional problems. In the medium term, very few options would be open. Firstly, the development schemes of the major national and multi-national manufacturing companies have already been determined both within the companies' internal corporate strategies and in their current understandings with existing central government departments and agencies. Secondly, in the petroleum industry the investment pattern that the off-shore companies have undertaken—or been committed to— would leave a Scottish administration no room to manoeuvre. Fields that have not yet started being developed could, of course, be delayed should a Scottish government wish to follow a policy of energy conservation on the Norwegian model. But it is doubtful that English claims to a say in their extraction and royalties could be ignored.

The substantial influence of economic devolution on Scottish industry would be two-fold. Scotland would be able to regenerate its industrial structure in terms which relate to its requirements rather than to those of the UK. Secondly, major efforts would be made to locate downstream petroleum processing plants in Scotland. There are no relevant cases that can be cited in order to attempt to assess the feasibility of such a massive integrated development; but certain factors—the availability of sites and labour, deep water close inshore for bulk carrier loading, established industrial markets in Scotland, the rest of the UK and accessible European and North American countries—suggest that Scotland holds major locational advantages which an autonomous Industry Department could exploit fully. But since the financing of such ventures is rarely a difficulty anywhere in the world, it is unlikely that the major corporations would single out Scotland. A structural downstream development policy would give Scotland an additional stable base for industrial development over the following decades.

England has certain claims over the rate of extraction of petroleum and royalties derived therefrom which must be respected. However, a Scottish administration would be able to control future developments. Oil revenues could provide a substantial balance for funding oil-related and non-oil related industrial restructuring, in much the same way as the UK government is relying on it now. A considerable proportion of such expenditures would have to support infrastructural developments, from roads to housing, to produce the conditions in which industry can thrive. The actual industry mix that might emerge—beyond petroleum-related ones—is a matter of speculation. In an expanding economy, certain existing industries would probably grow. Primary metal manufacture, food and drink, electronics and the 'traditional' specialised engineering industries are examples of the best placed. Other major industries such as textiles, clothing or paper-making will probably mark time.

However, the dynamics of expansion (ex-oil) will come from immigrant industries to whom Scotland offers real locational advantages in terms of natural resources as well as long established existing suppliers. These were well summarised in the 'Oceanspan' report of the Scottish Council (Development and Industry), which saw the central belt as part of a bridge between Europe and her commodity suppliers, with processing of materials taking place when local conditions—the availability of labour, water and other raw materials, energy, or sites—made it competitive.

There has been, as already mentioned, a change in management attitudes in industry; the prospects of future developments being prone to the vagaries of the cycle as has so often occurred since the war are low. The branch factory mentality is a disappearing phenomenon. The alternative, the continuation of the type of development strategy experienced since the war is probably not politically acceptable in

Scotland. The prospect of such a policy, coupled with a high rate of petroleum extraction and primary treatment, would not make the analyst confident of the emotional — let alone the economic — health of the nation in a generation's time.

10 PROSPECTS FOR TRANSPORT

Olaf Thornton

Scottish transport faces problems, some of which it shares with the rest of Britain and some of which are peculiar to Scotland. The big problem which underlies investment in most forms of transport in nearly all countries is the time scale. It is essentially long-term and from this flow a number of factors which present real problems when dealing with transport policy. Whether planning new motorways, bridges, railway electrification, port and harbour facilities or airports, each are in the field of long-range investment and large-scale investment. On any short-term time scale the planner would decide to do nothing at all for on a short-term view one could never justify a new motorway or an airport and yet such things have been essential in the past and will continue to be so. It is just that on the short-term the sums do not work out and seldom if ever can.

Governments are becoming more and more involved in decisions which vitally affect investment decisions in roads, railways, ports and aerodromes without which transport will stagnate. Governments are almost always over-persuaded by short-term considerations so that their decisions in essentially long-term matters have an inbuilt bias towards failure. This tendency to the short-term view is naturally heightened in times of economic stringency when cuts in the long-term potential minimise the short-term penalty and are easier and far less unpopular. For the long-term view to prevail, it has to be carried by some short-term advantage, winning votes, providing new jobs quickly, or saving existing ones for example. This seldom forms a good basis for long-term decisions.

The other grave disadvantage from which transport in general, suffers is that it is looked at and examined as discrete forms of transport called road, rail, air and water. This might be justifiable on purely economic grounds but transport has a large social factor as well. So long as different forms of transport are rivals, competing for limited resources, each with the idea that the more one gets the less there will be for the rest, the more distorted and confused the transport picture becomes. The criteria used for making judgements fluctuate widely for different forms of transport. Often there appear to be no objective criteria for judgement and instead only a collection of arguments assembled to justify a course of action already decided upon. A transport system for the country as a whole is seldom looked at. The rapid succession of Government encourage-ment and restraint for the economy has interfered with the nation's investment programme for transport far more than any commercial changes of pace in developments would have done. Heavy spending with little return has resulted to an extent unthinkable for private enterprise.

It is a tragedy that British Rail, commenting on the Government's transport policy Consultation Document must say, 'The only objectives at all clearly stated to the Board in the past have been financial; the lack of other defined objectives has been an important deficiency in the Board's planning process.'[1] These disadvantages are common to British Transport and are not peculiar to Scotland. The present set-up dictates a piece-meal approach based largely on short-term considerations; it results quite inevitably in a constantly changing view thereby ensuring a great waste of resources and preventing the country from reaping the potential rewards of any proper long-term plans.

To these basic disadvantages which British Transfort has to face must be added those peculiar to Scotland. The relative density of population and its distribution in Scotland compared to England is a long-term factor of importance and it places Scotland economically at a disadvan-tage. Scotland's population today is concentrated in the Central Belt with very large areas of low density population to the north and south of it. This east-west population axis is changing from its present Glasgow-Edinburgh axis to an Ayr-Aberdeen one, but even so there are likely to be very large areas of extremely low density population on either side of it for the forseeable future. Furthermore, Scotland has a very long indented coastline with many inhabited islands which present a transport problem quite unknown south of the border. The height of the land and its contours also present problems, the extent of which is often not appreciated by the general public. But in today's climate, particularly, Scottish problems are very secondary ones for British transport as a whole.

The view of the man or woman in the street is easily summarised: so far as public transport is concerned, he or she sees a deteriorating and increasingly expensive service. To the commuters on the London Under-ground, packed like sardines in a tin, it is quite incomprehensible that tube travel costs them more per mile than flying the Atlantic in Con-corde. Transport decisions appear to be taken at a distance by people who either do not know local conditions or who take scant notice of them. Nationalisation of public transport seems to have prevented enter-prise showing itself, if not killed it altogether, disregarded local conditions and put up fares while providing a worse service. Benefit to the public was the *raison d'etre* of public ownership and it has turned out to be largely illusory, though it need not have.

How far public criticism of transport is justified may be seen by examining the facts and figures. A good example of commuter rail fares was quoted during a debate in Parliament early in 1976.[2] It was the cost of an annual season ticket from Faversham to London, a journey of less than fifty miles.

	£
At the beginning of 1975 it cost	234
During January 1975 it rose to	263
In May it increased to	327
In September it went up to	375
The latest increase at the time of the debate put it up to	447

The fare rose from £234 to £447 in just over a year. The second class single rail fare from Glasgow to London was £5.70 in May 1970 and by May 1976 it was £15. Of course the examples quoted are not the end of the matter. Public transport by road and sea presents a similar and equally depressing picture of higher fares, higher subsidies and a deteriorating service.

It is more difficult to give concise and telling examples of deterioration of service than of fares increases but, with the exception of Inter-City rail services, the public is convinced that passenger services by both road and rail have undoubtedly deteriorated. Inter-City rail is claimed to be profitable and it is generally recognised as having improved its standard of service, but in Scotland, deprived of an Inter-City network comparable to that in England, benefits are confined to Edinburgh and Glasgow. This is explained by the wider population spread in Scotland underlining the real differences north and south of the border. The public feeling that local conditions are ignored and that transport decisions taken far away are very real but more difficult to quantify. Such feelings often arouse emotions that have little or nothing to do with transport. It is worth probing a little further to see how much substance there is.

In a centralised economy local transport executives, though much better informed of regional conditions, face a considerable handicap in participating in policy formulation. While top management are concentrated at headquarters, their close daily contact inevitably leads to decision-making by a head office consensus. The odds are heavily against a local view prevailing if it is in any way counter to the head office consensus. Efforts by local management at closer contact with head office lead to less association with the region and eventual cooption by the head office ensues. The nationalised industries have another big hurdle which makes the Regional Chairman's task very nearly impossible, in the shape of the influence of Ministers and senior Civil Servants, concentrated in London. The subjective judgements of politicians masquerading as the public interest are unpredictable and constantly changing, even for those living in daily contact with this flux of expediency, for the Regional Chairman it is the last straw.

There is undoubtedly a very heavy anti-local bias and in so far as the man in the street senses this intuitively, he is correct. On some occasions the wider, less parochial view of the more remote headquarters may be wiser and better informed than the local opinion, but so far as local considerations go, it is a disadvantage if the headquarters are outside the area in which they operate. In the case of Scotland, it matters little whether the headquarters are in London or anywhere else in England. The present system of nationalisation has added extra problems since it was continual Government interference based largely on short-term considerations which have been subject to constant changes.

The chart in Figure 1 is a simplification of how responsibility for transport works. Even though simplified, it can only be described as a mess. It is often even more difficult for a layman to read an organisation chart than a company balance sheet. On the face of it, it may seem easy enough to understand, even if it is somewhat complicated, but what is not easy to see are the implications that lie behind it.

The chart shows that different forms of transport make their own case for what they want to do. If it involves large sums of public money, it is inevitably viewed with great suspicion by other transport interests because there is always the fear that more money for one form of transport means less for another. This ensures that there will be no unified transport approach. It also makes it easier for the Government either to say 'No', or, more often, to cut down the amount of money that they are willing to authorise. It is very much a case of divide and rule and it is unlikely to be changed without a struggle because it is a situation that suits the administration.

Politically it is disastrous to take any long term decisions, since these reap all the short-term disadvantages and are unlikely to stand long enough to prove themselves. The people who are running a particular form of transport are forced first to arrive at priorities and then to present them in whatever form has the best chance of being accepted. If they do not operate in this way they are never likely to achieve anything at all. The reasons why they decide that they want to do something

TRANSPORT AND GOVERNMENT

CABINET OFFICE

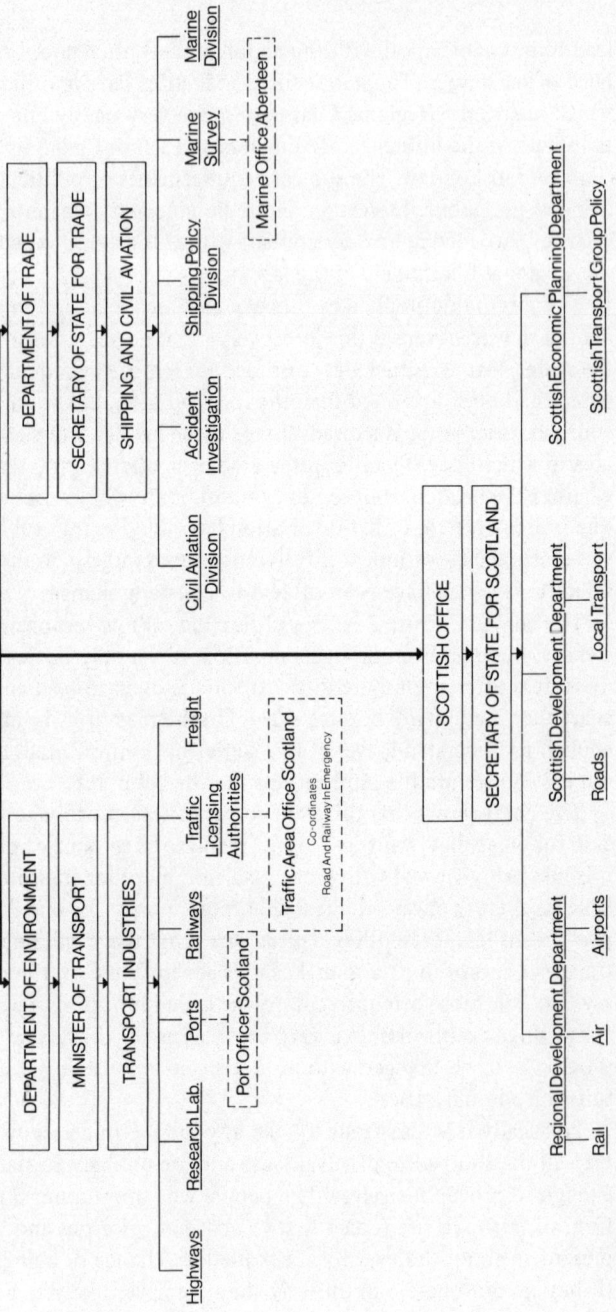

DEPARTMENT OF ENVIRONMENT

MINISTER OF TRANSPORT

TRANSPORT INDUSTRIES

Highways — Research Lab — Ports — Railways — Traffic Licensing Authorities — Freight

Port Officer Scotland

Traffic Area Office Scotland
Co-ordinates Road And Railway In Emergency

DEPARTMENT OF TRADE

SECRETARY OF STATE FOR TRADE

SHIPPING AND CIVIL AVIATION

Civil Aviation Division — Accident Investigation — Shipping Policy Division — Marine Survey — Marine Division

Marine Office Aberdeen

SCOTTISH OFFICE

SECRETARY OF STATE FOR SCOTLAND

Regional Development Department

Rail — Air — Airports

Scottish Development Department

Roads — Local Transport

Scottish Economic Planning Department

Scottish Transport Group Policy

and the reasons advanced in the case put forward for approval are often quite different, but because acceptance by the Government is the crucial test, they have to play the political game, which is quite different from either the business game or the scientific game. The rules of all three are fundamentally different, though this is often not appreciated by the general public.

The scientist publishes his research results in a form that can be verified by others quite independently. There is no point in trying to bias the conclusions by selecting some evidence and suppressing other evidence. Still less is there any point in fudging the results or presenting spurious calculations because he will be found out and exposed as a charlatan. Thus there is an inbuilt bias towards truth in scientific research, not because scientists are more moral than other people, but because of the nature of scientific research. In politics, the opposite is unfortunately the case. The short term view predominates and in the short term one is judged not on verifiable facts but on the promises made and how convincing they sound.

The business test is clumsy but in the end generally effective, when free from Government interference, with bankruptcy as an ultimate sanction. This prospect is real and usually engenders a sense of realism. The business safeguard is often lacking or inappropriate in nationalised or municipal undertakings, nor unfortunately is there any adequate alternative to take its place. Transport, like many nationalised undertakings, combines major social and economic factors with no clear guidelines from the Government. Short of bankrupting the nation, no effective control of Government opinion exists, so that management is often hamstrung by political and wildly fluctuating interference. The really astounding thing is that able men accept the chairmanship of nationalised industries. The Department which vets any proposed expenditure will, of course, be highly suspicious of any case put forward, however honestly prepared, although it is not usually in a good position to shout it down, provided that it has not been blatantly over-stated. This is the position which British Rail face.

Roads are in a different, and up to now altogether more favourable, position. In general, they can get away with spending vast sums of money without the sort of economic justification demanded of British Rail. The A9 Perth to Inverness road upgrading at £60 million went through with ease, compared to the battle to put the Perth to Inverness railway back to standard at £3.7 million, even though much of this cost was only restoring the Beeching cuts that with hindsight looked shortsighted. Did anyone ever examine the relative financial value of the two proposals?

British Rail may have done so, but if they did, it is doubtful whether much weight was attached to it. Many uneconomic railway lines have had to close, but are uneconomic roads put to the same test? It would appear that the rules are quite different for different forms of transport. These are some of the factors which lie behind the transport organisation showing how much the organisation chart fails to reveal.

It is perhaps surprising that the Government should have produced a consultation document on Transport Policy[3] at all and it is greatly to their credit that they have done so. It is easy to criticise the document and even if many of the criticisms are real and fundamental, they should not be allowed to obscure the fact that to have such a document in itself is a great advance. Paragraph 5.4.6 of the Consultative Document is most encouraging where it clearly states the Government's intention to undertake an early study of the future long term demand for and provision of public passenger transport for inter-urban journeys with particular emphasis on the strategy to be pursued by road, rail and air. Why this enlightened approach should be confined to inter-city journeys and why it is not applicable to goods traffic also remains a mystery. Unfortunately the Consultative Document concentrates on today's problems and the present state of the nation's economy. It dismisses further rail electrification as an alternative to oil and it does not even give wholehearted acceptance of current EEC regulations on road transport.

The document shows no sign of Government recognition for the time scale in which transport policy decisions should be taken. To take short term views of what is essentially a long term problem can only lead to further deterioration of our transport in general and our railways in particular, which will still further unbalance the transport systems of the country as a whole. It will almost certainly place Scotland in a relatively worse position within Britain than it is today. These are extremely serious and very real possibilities for Scotland and must not go unchallenged.

Other less obvious factors are done less than justice by the Government's Consultative Document. Road deaths in Britain are of the order of a Flixborough explosion every thirty-six hours, but, of course, are far less dramatic. Oil is one of the biggest single factors in our balance of payments deficit. North Sea oil is expensive to extract and difficult to protect. Its working life is perhaps no more than thirty years and it is certainly limited. World oil reserves are a finite resource and the time is approaching when it will have to be restricted mainly to constructive uses such as petro-chemical industry and its burning in furnaces or engines severely curtailed. Electricity will supply a growing proportion of our overall power requirements, however generated, and this will have a profound effect on transport from about the year 2,000 onwards. Pollution is a growing problem and because its effect is cumulative, will become a very much more serious one. Noise, dirt, vibration, social disturbance and city congestion are difficult to put into an economic equation, but are none the less real.

British Rail has a High Speed Train and an Advanced Passenger Train. The HST can travel at 125 mph and is running between London and Bristol. It does the journey in 1 hour 25 minutes, a saving of 21 minutes over the previous time. The APT could travel at 150 mph but is limited to 125 mph because of signalling difficulties, so why bother with the APT at all? One of the facts is that on the London/Glasgow run the HST could only save a few minutes on the present 5 hours. The APT will cut 5 hours to 4 hours. The reason is geography. The HST has to slow down for curves, whereas the APT with its ingenious tilting suspension can corner much faster. In other words, geography means that Scotland could benefit far more from the introduction of the APT than many parts of Britain, and if a shortsighted view prevails, it is the APT that is in most danger, and if the APT is cancelled it is Scotland once again that will get the worst of the deal.

Self-imposed rules and practices for transport ensure a worsening system and make it most unlikely that any real initiative will be allowed to develop. Apart from the fact that for over five years no rail investment plan has lasted longer than six months, the late Chairman of British Rail is quoted as saying that he has suffered from a 'total lack of clarity of the Board's objectives'[4] and consistency on the part of the Government. British Rail compares poorly with the best examples overseas. In France they are planning the new Tres Grande Vitesse (TGV) with a completely new track from Paris to Lyon, a distance of 255 miles, which will take just 2 hours. The TGV will have a maximum speed of 160 mph. In freight wagon utilisation in thousands of ton/kilometres per annum, Britain compares badly:

British Rail	68
Germany	235
France	315

(Figures for 1970)

Another pointer is to look at the number of private sidings:

Britain	2,200
France	11,000

The Sunday Times of 1 April 1976 had an interesting article about William B. Johnston, who is an acknowledged expert on railways. He runs the Illinois Central Gulf Railway, which has roughly the same track mileage, the same freight loadings and passenger figures as British Rail, but has one-tenth of the staff and since 1966 has generated pre-tax profits of more than £200 million. His comment was,

> Poor Dick Marsh has responsibility without power . . . He knows how to run a railway but he is just not allowed to . . . I told him as I was leaving that I thought he had a great future in the States.

I am very far from advocating that we copy everything that Johnston has done but it is clear that there is a lot to learn from outside Britain. It appears that Britain has three choices: accept the trend towards the private car as inevitable and providing more and more roads whilst allowing other forms of transport to decline which is what is happening now as the traffic figures for both freight and passengers in Scotland show:

	Road freight %	Rail freight %	Water freight %
1960	52	36	12
1975	72	17	11

	Car passengers %	Bus passengers %	Rail passengers %
1960	42	50	8
1975	74	19	7

An alternative would be to stop building new roads, let the traffic snarl up and literally force people to find other ways of moving about, or there might be a conscious attempt at an integrated transport system for Scotland which would involve making plans to change the present transport pattern by making public transport a more desirable alternative for many people and also more attractive for many freight users.

The first alternative leaves the less well-off without transport. At present about half of all households in Britain have no car and even on present trends a quarter will still have no car by the year 2000. It will damage both town and country and will use up scarce agricultural land. It will restrict mobility for many and retard the matching of jobs and people in relation to the problems of long term oil supplies, pollution and death on the roads. The second alternative of doing nothing is not acceptable in the present political climate. The third alternative implies that Britain as a whole is willing to change. Two most important changes must be faced if it is to become possible. First management must be given a real chance to do a good job and if it fails it must be replaced.

To do this it is essential to define the job to be done, for without this there is no yardstick against which to measure their performance. Secondly, decision-making must be brought closer to the area served and made more manageable.

No plan or organisation will guarantee success but some attempted solutions do guarantee failure. The way forward that offers the opportunity of success is to put all transport in Scotland, including the provision of roads under one Scottish Transport Authority. It should be independent of any British Transport Authority and independent of both Westminster and a Scottish Assembly in the short term. It could never be completely independent of Government because it spends public money but it could have the sort of independence that the BBC has. It could not be immune from cuts in a time of financial crisis but it would at least be as free from government interference as is broadcasting and it is not beyond the wit of man to devise such a new form of public ownership for transport. The total sum of money for Scottish Transport including that required for roads in so far as they are at present provided by the Exchequer would be available for an integrated transport system. How it should be divided up between one form of transport and another and what should be developed would be their decision. Such an authority would require subsidiary Boards but they would have far more real power than the present Board of British Rail. Both the subsidiary Boards and the Scottish Transport Authority should be located in Scotland.

Such a transport organisation would create the opportunity for consistent long term planning and would enable Scottish Transport to be considered as a whole placing responsibility and power in the same hands. By being based in Scotland, it would be less remote and by being confined to Scotland, it would be far more manageable. The psychological significance of such a step would be sufficient to liberate new ideas as well as a new hope for the future.

Notes

1. *Transport Policy, an Opportunity for Change: Comments by the British Railways Board on the Transport Policy Consultative Document,* 1976.
2. *Hansard,* vol. 903, no. 33, 'Debate on Transport Policy', 23 Jan. 1976.
3. *Transport Policy Consultative Document,* vols. 1 and 2, HMSO, April 1976.
4. Sir Richard Marsh reported in *The Times,* 16 March 1976.

11 THE BUILT ENVIRONMENT

Jan Fladmark

'Built environment' is used here in a broad sense, not just referring to buildings but also embracing the way buildings come together to form the man-made fabric of towns and cities where people live, work, and enjoy themselves. With this broad concept in mind, let us then look around and ask ourselves whether what is being built in Scotland today represents something that is uniquely Scottish. The answer must be *no*, because it is becoming increasingly difficult to ascribe features to the built environment of any particular country that gives it an identity of its own. This is in large measure due to the emergence of a modern building technology using methods and materials which are uniform over large parts of the world. It is most strikingly evident in the urban environment where the same kind of modern structures can be seen in cities like Hamburg, Paris, and Naples as those which reach skywards in Glasgow, Edinburgh and Dundee. As well as building form and construction, the approach to environmental planning is also similar. The word may differ with language; but the phenomenon known as 'motorways' in Britain look the same, and assume the same significance, to modern man wherever he belongs. The image of Scotland's contemporary built environment, therefore, has little in it that makes it stand out in contrast to that of any other European country.

To find a particularly Scottish identity it is necessary to go back to the vernacular form of building which continued as a distinctly national tradition well into the second half of the nineteenth century if not longer. Although a great deal of destruction has taken place in the name of progress, much of it survives, and it is very different from that found elsewhere, even south of the Border. The predominant Scottish building material was stone, quarried locally giving regional variations in texture and colour. Although stone was used throughout the British Isles, the English refined the use of fired clay bricks to a much larger extent than the Scots. As the half-timbered Elizabethan house with brick in-fill is the hallmark of the English building tradition, so the sturdy stone houses with crowstepped gables and skew putts in the fishing villages of East Fife are the epitome of the Scottish vernacular. The use of stone and the vernacular style continued in the typical Scottish tenements which sprouted up in expanding towns during the industrial revolution and after, whereas contemporary English housing was more commonly erected in brick.

Like any broad generalisation, the comparison may not convince every reader, but it can at least be argued that it is from the vernacular part of our built environment that we derive a distinctly Scottish identity. When it comes to contemporary building, it is no longer possible to distinguish between one country and another in terms of building materials, methods of construction, and form. The answer can to some extent be found in that there is now a greater emphasis on *movement* than on *belonging*: that is people care more about their ability to travel to work, for shopping, and for leisure, than they do for the community and the immediate environment of their home and work. In looking for the shape of things to come, therefore, the most promising aspect to explore might be the way decisions are made about major factors which cause change in our built environment. The decision-making process is complex (see Figure 1) with people playing inter-dependent roles in many different capacities: elected representatives interact with technical officers, local government interact with central departments, and ordinary citizens and voluntary pressure groups may contribute through public participation.

Current literature on environmental questions abounds with jargon such as think tank, scenario, extrapolation, futurology, and many others. In essence they are all 'crystal ball gazing', and on the environmental front there are broadly two kinds of participants: those who are concerned with crystal ball gazing for its own sake, and those who actually attempt to use it through the decision-making process of our planning system. The former is a fascinating occupation, the latter extremely hazardous and fraught with difficulty. It has been said that trend projections all have one common denominator: they are all likely to be wrong. Assuming that planners are concerned with resolving competing demands on resources and remembering that the time horizons of planning often extend far into the future, it is not surprising that their dependence on trend predictions has made them easy scapegoats for the various environmental lobbies.

It can safely be said that Scotland emerged from the relatively inactive period of the 1950s as a leader in the field of environmental planning. The very act of creating the Scottish Development Department in 1962, with a very wide range of environmental functions, was a pioneering venture. For the first time in British institutional history a single central government department existed to ensure proper integration of such closely related functions as local government, housing, planning,

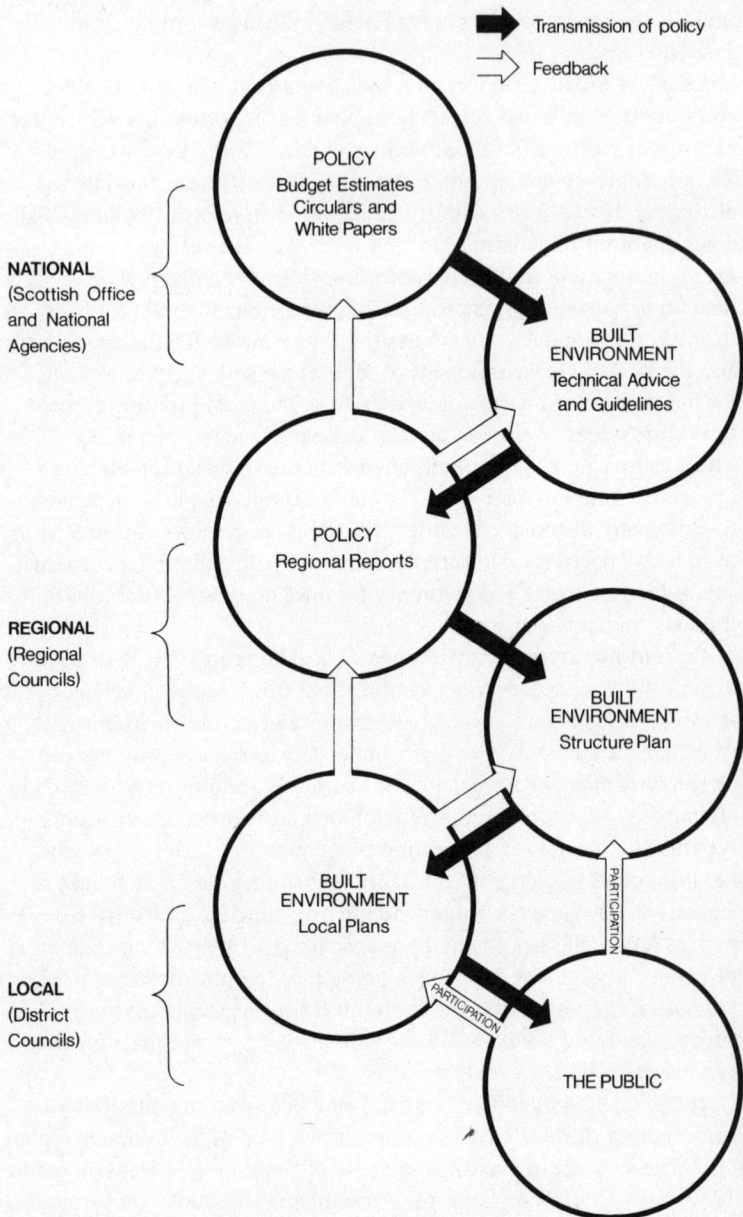

Figure 1. Hierarchical policy-making process for the built environment.

public utilities, and some years later, roads. The English followed suit about ten years later by creating the Department of the Environment. But south of the Border this process of integration was reversed in 1976 by separating the roads function and establishing a new Ministry of Transport.

The planning policies to be pursued by the new Development Department were incorporated in the White Paper of 1963 entitled 'Central Scotland: a programme for development and growth' (Cmnd. 2188). As an exercise in planning this document was not only advanced in that it set out a comprehensive programme of capital investment, but it also attempted to translate that programme into spatial terms by specifying the geographical locations for new and expanded communities, selected sites for industrial development, and extensions of the road network. Having thus established a framework for planning at national level, the Government in partnership with local authorities proceeded to prepare a series of *advisory* regional plans. Four years later there was another White Paper entitled the 'Scottish Economy 1965-70' (Cmnd. 2864), and it too was followed by several regional studies. In these exercises an attempt was being made to integrate physical and economic aspects of planning, and strategic thinking at both national and regional levels. These were new and remarkable achievements for a part of the UK then generally referred to as being backward.

By 1974 advisory regional plans had been prepared for almost the entire area of Scotland, and the series culminated in that year by publication of the 'West Central Scotland Plan' which included the Glasgow conurbation: the largest single urban population concentration in Scotland with 2.5 million people. The situation in the West had been that the 'Greater Glasgow Transportation Study' was completed in 1968 paving the way for implementation of a gigantic urban motorway system for the city. Like all studies of that ilk, it was solely concerned with the design of a highway system, and land use and people were merely seen in terms of their capacity to generate traffic. Unhappily this amounted to a 'cart before the horse' situation, because it was only in 1974 with publication of the West Central Scotland Plan that an integrated planning approach to the built environment of the region emerged, embracing land use and transportation along with an equal concern for social, economic, and cultural issues. The study concluded that rehabilitation of the inner city should be given high priority, but the recommendations came too late. Tragically, by this time vast areas of old Glasgow had been demolished in anticipation of the advancing urban motorway system. The West Central Scotland Plan was particularly significant because its authors were among the first planners in Scotland to respond to changing demographic and economic circumstances.

Although the 'East Central Scotland Land Use Transportation Study' had also been completed in 1968, the local authorities in the area could not agree among themselves to a joint scheme for implementation. Allocated budget estimates by the Secretary of State were not taken up, and the delays carried on into a period of greater economic stringency and a different climate of public opinion. Edinburgh was thus saved from the kind of wholesale destruction experienced in Glasgow, due to historical circumstances rather than to any deliberate action on the part of decision-makers.

The end of the 1960s also saw the introduction to Scotland of a series of new agencies concerned with environmental questions at an intermediate level between central and local government, these being the Countryside Commission for Scotland, the Scottish Tourist Board, and the Scottish Sports Council. The Highlands and Islands Development Board was created at this time, but it belongs in a special category because its brief only covers part of Scotland. Along with the institutional innovations there was a shift away from the comprehensive policy statements embodied in the two White Papers. The 1969 White Paper on 'Scottish Roads in the 1970s' (Cmnd. 3953, a last Scottish compliment to Beeching's policy for rail closures) was the beginning of an approach related to single functional questions and special problem areas, altogether more flexible. A subsequent example being the 'Coastal Planning Guidelines' produced in 1974 by the Development Department in response to the environmental pressures created by North Sea oil and gas developments. The discussion document on a 'Park System for Scotland' by the Countryside Commission for Scotland in 1974 and the policy statement on 'Tourism and Recreation' by the Scottish Tourist Board in 1975 were also cases of policy initiatives related to functional responsibilities.

The fact that national policy formulation was moving out from central departments to include the new agencies was a very significant development in constitutional terms. It represented a widening of participation by bodies with a greater freedom from the conventional constraints imposed on departments by the principle of ministerial responsibility. Although some detractors may say that the proliferation of new agencies has led to confusion and much overlapping of work, there is evidence to suggest that a great deal of inter-agency coordination is taking place, and the opportunity for flexibility with speed of action is likely to outweigh any disadvantages.[1]

The policy-making process as a whole is based on a two-way reciprocal flow of information which is important for several reasons. Details of local implementations may have significant technical implications on national and regional strategy, and the degree of public participation tends to be more intense at local than at higher levels. Furthermore the statutory mechanism for implementation is generally controlled by the lower levels, while the flow of funds is regulated through the upper level by Treasury control, ensuring a fairly even balance of power between central and local government.

Where do decisions come from and who makes them? The question is frequently asked and whether the concern is with the built environment or not, Figure 1 goes some way towards providing an answer. The 'policy' box at national level represents budget estimates and government circulars expressing ministerial policy, while the 'built environment' represents aspects of policy with a strong concern for land use implications such as the documents on Coastal Planning Guidelines and a Park System for Scotland. The two White Papers referred to earlier do not easily fall into either box, and they partially cover both because they contain investment policy as well as a spatial expression of that policy. The middle and lower levels of the diagram reflect the new two-tier system of local government introduced in 1975.[2] At regional level the 'policy' box represents the *regional report* and the built environment is covered by the *structure plan*. At the district level the boxes represent *local plans* and the procedures built into the system for public participation.

In the 1960s, when only two levels of government existed, there was no means for effective decision-making at regional level, and it was to fill this vacuum that the advisory regional plans were prepared. An ad hoc system of advisory planning committees were set up, in each case representing all the local authorities in the area to be covered by the plan. The committee produced a corporate policy statement representing the planning brief, and the advisory plan in turn became the land use expression of that brief for the built environment. At local level the individual planning authorities determined policy within the framework of the advisory plans, and that policy was then translated into the old style development plans.

An aspect of crucial importance for coming to grips with future trends is first an understanding of the underlying assumptions used as a basis for planning. The general theme of the 1960s was growth; population projections indicated that there would be an increase in the UK of about 20 million by the end of the century and an abundant supply of oil from the Third World to provide cheap petrol. This combined with a rapidly expanding car industry led us to believe that we were likely to approach the high rates of private car ownership experienced in the USA.[3]

The expected increase in population resulted in a search for urban expansion opportunities. It is interesting to note for example that many of the regional plans from the 1960s had words like growth, expansion, and development potential in their titles. Although the additional numbers of people were due to natural increase (difference in births over deaths) within the large conurbations and major cities, these areas were considered to be congested and already too large, and the solution generally chosen was to find sites for new communities (new towns and town expansion schemes) in relatively sparsely populated areas which could offer a better living environment as well as improved employment opportunities. Having chosen the broad policy objective, the next consideration was to decide how best to carry out the detailed planning of the distribution and the layout of the new communities. The plans which emerged showed a distinct preference for low density and a rather dispersed form of development, undoubtedly due to a dislike for old style tenements as well as many unfortunate experiences with modern high rise residential blocks.[4]

The second assumption in the growth hypothesis related to personal mobility. The residential suburbs which spread around the towns as a consequence of the industrial revolution were closely related to a system of public transport made possible by the development of railways, but by the 1960s people had begun in a really big way to enjoy a new kind of mobility. Incomes were rising and cars were becoming so cheap that no sections of the community were excluded. In terms of infrastructure services, therefore, it was considered safe to assume that railways and other forms of public transport were a thing of the past, and in future people would rely on the private motor car for travel to work, shopping and recreation. In 1963 Scotland had 83 miles of dual carriageway trunk roads, including motorways, and by 1973 the mileage had been increased to 265. For railways the figure stood at 6,544 miles of track in 1963, and that was reduced to 3,656 miles by 1973.[5]

In the case of Cumbernauld, for instance, a new town was planned almost entirely around the principle of full car ownership. Livingston New Town was designated to lie close to the main lines of communication between Glasgow and Edinburgh with the attendant consequences that might have on future travel patterns. Although the first consultants planned the layout so that the built-up area straddled one of the then operational railway lines, the town centre was designed to be served entirely by road transport and is located too far away from the track to make passenger services by rail a practical proposition should the need arise.[6] The work done by Scottish planners during the 1960s was second to none in technical competence, and was furthermore a fair response to the environmental policy objectives set by politicians and society generally. The crucial question now, however, is whether both planners and the planned are capable of adjusting quickly enough to the radically changed circumstances of the present.

The growth hypothesis is falling apart;[7] if current trends continue there may soon be zero population growth and this will have significant environmental consequences. To start with it will be necessary to examine the policy regarding new communities because there just will not be enough people to meet their population targets without serious detriment to the social and economic fabric of existing towns and cities. The recent argument between the Strathclyde Region and Stonehouse Development Corporation is more about who will get the people than about who is allocated the scarce monetary resources presently available for investment to create more employment. The population of the area covered by the West Central Scotland Plan fell from 2,525,000 in 1962 to 2,482,000 in 1972. A reduction of 43,000 people over eleven years in spite of the natural increase for the region having been constantly above the national average since 1951. The most disturbing aspect of the situation is that the population level in the inner areas of Glasgow is beginning to fall below that planned for within the massive urban renewal schemes. Since the early 1950s at least 200,000 people from central Glasgow have been rehoused on the edge of the city, and a total population of 120,000 now live in the new towns of East Kilbride, Cumbernauld and Irvine. It is not surprising therefore that the Government has decided to abandon the plan for Stonehouse. Similar arguments took place at the beginning of 1976 between the Lothian Region and Livingston New Town when the Regional Report was being prepared, and earlier between London and the surrounding counties.

What about the other main factor in the growth hypothesis: car ownership rates? At the height of the recent energy crisis it was widely thought that the impact would be immediate and severe. In terms of impact on environ~   ~licy the situation in Edinburgh does well as an example. No sooner had Colin Buchanan and Partners as consultants completed their plan based on Buchanan's own well established assumption that growth in the number of cars is inevitable, when a local professor was able to demonstrate that the city could have a public transport system based on rail and buses without the expense and devastation of new roads: the energy situation simply indicated that the cars might not be there to use the proposed new roads anyway.[8] Nevertheless it now seems certain that as long as oil is being extracted and crude is being refined for various industrial purposes Scotland will continue to have fairly plentiful supplies of relatively cheap petrol as a by-product.

The unpleasant truth however is that oil is not a renewable resource and is likely to be depleted within the life of the next generation, and the question of impact is therefore more a matter of timing than of degree. Because the energy crisis has subsided it is tempting to continue a policy of urban dispersal without adequate regard to the future provision of public transport services. As a matter of urgency Stockholm's example which never abandoned the principle of the Victorians who extended the residential suburbs along the lines of their railway network should be followed.[9] All the cars could be taken from the roads in Stockholm tomorrow and the city would still continue to function.

The displaced people generally represented low income groups who have been re-housed in large suburban estates or in new communities on green field sites as at Glasgow. This has introduced long journeys to work—distances likely to cause hardship when greater transportation costs begin to bite, and there is likely to be strong pressure to move back, which in turn may lead to social conflict because the tendency has been for members of the middle classes to re-populate some of the more fashionable residential areas near the city centres. The Southside of Edinburgh is an interesting example of the attempts of displaced people to move back to the city. The area formed part of an urban renewal scheme jointly prepared by Edinburgh Corporation and the University, and the population of the Southside which had been 12,000 in 1951 was down to less than 5,000 by 1973. The scheme was only partially implemented and large areas of empty tenements remain. With the greater emphasis on conservation during the last few years, housing associations have been formed to rehabilitate some of the better properties. At least one such association has members who were former residents of the Southside and who are now living in suburban estates. If this initiative of moving back gathers momentum it indicates that the kind of built environment preferred by many today is rather different from that which has been provided in recent times both by public and private sectors.

To provide an acceptable built environment in years to come it is necessary for dispersal to stop and for there to be a concentration on improving the existing urban fabric. Recent ministerial pronouncements playing down new town development and stressing the need for re-vitalisation of inner city areas seem to indicate that the process of change has already started. The danger is, however, that this focussing on the central areas of cities will result in further destruction, because there is still a great deal of momentum behind the 'demolish and rebuild' syndrome.

Sir Robert Grieve's observation that 'the traditional Glasgow tenement is best defined as a vertical crofting community' extends the argument about environmental identity to embrace social dimensions. Grieve, the grand old man of modern Scottish town planning who had been raised in these very tenements, was attempting to say that the community that existed in the old tenement areas was as strong in kinship ties, mutual self-help, and solidarity in the face of adversity as were the crofting communities in the North East Highlands. The removal of the old physical fabric is therefore not just a matter of destroying a visual identity but it also amounts to weakening Scotland's traditional urban community.

The economic arguments between renewal and rehabilitation are not yet settled, but the lobby in favour of conservation is growing stronger and it would be fair to say that the case against rehabilitation is gradually being dismantled. Maintenance of old buildings is as a rule cheaper than that of new structures, and if the social cost of community disintegration is added to renewal, there should be little scope for doubt when choosing options for future action. There will always be a need for new buildings, but for these the vernacular tradition just as much as the various schools of modern architecture should be turned to. It is entirely feasible within the limits of modern building technology to demonstrate greater sensitivity to *fit* between old and new, and the traditional principles of siting and layout according to climate and the grain of the land. It defies comprehension why the 'hilltop-town' principle should have been adopted for Cumbernauld in a windswept country where settlements traditionally have been located on sheltered sites. The procedures of the 1947 Town Planning Act were designed to achieve comprehensive redevelopment of the decaying urban environment normally found in the inner areas of old cities. They started showing results on the ground during the 1960s. But unfortunately, they have tended to destroy some of the more attractive old environments of both historical interest and social significance, causing massive commercial developments and the removal of people from the central areas.

The average level of car ownership for the United Kingdom as a whole is 0.25 cars per person while the equivalent rate for Scotland is only 0.20 cars. This may seem a small difference, but it is sufficient to merit consideration for environmental policy because a better balance must be achieved in future between car ownership rates and the planned provision for those who have to rely on public transport. Glasgow represents a striking example of current double-thinking: the city has been receiving a relatively high level of investment on road building per head of population yet the average rate of car ownership in Glasgow is only 0.165 cars per person.

The immediate task ahead, for Scotland, is to review existing plans, remembering that the regional strategies prepared during the 1960s were designed with growth targets related to the anticipated increase in population: then estimated to amount to another 20 million people by the year 2000 in the United Kingdom as a whole. A great deal of investment has already been made in anticipation of this massive growth, and the first step should be to find out where over-provision of facilities exists. The over-provision is likely to be found in the form of surplus capacities, particularly in the new towns, and the next step would be to set these against perceived deficiencies in service provision within the regions. Rather than being seen as self-sufficient communities catering for their own needs they can thus become meaningful providers of services within their regional setting. In cases where over-provision is still found to exist after this kind of regional analysis, it would be a matter of choosing alternative users for surplus accommodation.

Probably the greatest asset of Scotland's built environment is its setting of extensive and largely unspoilt countryside. The forethought of an earlier generation of planners has kept it intact right up to the boundaries of our major towns in the form of green belts.[10] The continuation of this policy and two more recent policy initiatives provide the protective underpinning for an acceptable future. The other two are the 'Coastal Planning Guidelines' and 'A Park System for Scotland'. The former identifies the parts of our coast that constitute a heritage worthy of protection, and the latter outlines a hierarchy of parks that takes into account local, regional and national needs. If the natural heritage is to be preserved, it will be necessary to integrate these three strands of thinking into a coherent and coordinated management policy that embraces the urban fringe, fragile upland landscape, and the coast.

A great proportion of Scotland's economic riches will come from the North Sea during the next few decades, putting great pressures on the coast line. There is a great temptation to accept development on the grounds that it will create much needed employment, but sight should not be lost of the fact that industries associated with oil in particular tend to be capital intensive. It is only in the construction phase of development that a large labour force is required, and unless our scenario is well balanced there may be a large footloose and itinerant labour force building plants in places which eventually will be manned by a few highly skilled technicians. Scotland may have achieved the desired productive capacity, but unless it is careful the natural heritage may be irrepairably damaged and the problem of unemployment will remain. The Norwegians have seen with alarm people being drawn from more traditional activities into better paid oil-related employment, and realising the difficulties of re-establishing the traditional forms of employment they have now decided to handle only the oil required for the domestic market and the surplus is exported in its crude state for refining elsewhere. A selfish attitude it may be, but one that will bring long term benefits to both the natural and built environment in Norway.

One of the many threats to Scotland's upland landscape is an insatiable appetite for energy consumption. Although it is widely recognised that current generating capacity of electricity is adequate to meet general need, there is the problem of meeting peak demands. The generating methods normally used are not sufficiently responsive to cope with fluctuations in loading on the grid and there is pressure on the generating industry to provide additional pumped storage hydro-electric stations which can function in accordance with the demand cycle. The latest proposal for a station of this type is in one of the most precious upland landscapes at Craigroyston on Loch Lomondside, and many would share Thomas Huxley's reservations about the justification of the scheme just 'to get extra electricity into the grid for the six o'clock tea'.[11]

It is the underlying attitude to demand rather than the locational disadvantages that is objectionable in the Craigroyston case, and if we are to provide a built environment that will suit the needs and aspirations of future generations it will be necessary to break out of the inertia of current approaches. Thus Scotland should develop alternative sources of energy for domestic use and adopt more appropriate forms of technology for building purposes. It has come as a big surprise to many that it is possible in our overcast climate to use solar panels for heating domestic hot water. It has long been known that it is a practical proposition in sunnier climates for purpose built houses, but over the last few years it has been demonstrated that solar panels can be effective even when installed on the existing roofs of tenement buildings in Scotland. Although wind power is still to be re-discovered as a practical means of generating electricity, feasibility studies have shown that the wind climate of Tiree would be capable of operating a district heating unit that could produce 700,000 kilowatt hours of electricity in a year.[12]

These developments fall broadly within the terms of *appropriate technology* which is a familiar concept in many parts of the Third World. It simply means the use of methods that are generally more labour intensive and based on local raw materials than is the case with the capital intensive and highly mechanised techniques of industrialised nations. As well as developing alternative sources of energy, priority should also be given to research and development of appropriate technology and a greater degree of self help in building the man-made environment. The use of local labour and local materials would encourage regional variations and may encourage a greater sensitivity to the surviving heritage in both the natural and built environment. The kind of change I have in mind can perhaps best be illustrated by referring to what is already happening in the baking industry. The large companies have for a long time operated with a few really large production units serviced by fleets of vans distributing their standard range of products to local retail outlets. Due to a combination of increased transportation costs and changing tastes among the public, some firms have decentralised production to the individual retail outlets, thus harnessing local talent to produce bread with exciting regional variations in smell, taste and texture.

It can be argued that few of the problems discussed are confined to Scotland alone and the solutions may therefore turn out to be similar to those adopted elsewhere. In fact the prospects in Scotland are just as dependent on good timing as on the type of response, and it is my belief that Scotland is in a better position to respond quickly to the new circumstances than anywhere else in the United Kingdom. I say this on the basis of the following considerations:

1. A branch of central government administration is located in Edinburgh with responsibility for environmental questions. This brings central government close to Scottish problems and allows specifically Scottish policies to be pursued at national level. The proposed Scottish Assembly would reinforce this further.
2. Scotland has more effective regional authorities than south of the Border. Their areas are defined more functionally and they are fewer in number, thus making it easier to plan comprehensively and to co-ordinate across boundaries.
3. Unlike England and Wales who are relying entirely on development plans still covering a period of 20 years, Scotland has an additional tool of environmental decision-making in the 'regional reports'. These

are intended to be simple but comprehensive documents covering a relatively short period of one to five years allowing more frequent interaction on environmental policy between the regions and central departments.

4. The large number of regional plans prepared for various parts of the country during the 1960s provided planners and elected representatives both with *knowledge* and *experience* of how to deal with environmental problems. If the dictum that 'wisdom is knowledge tempered by experience' still applies there is nothing to fear from the new local authorities.

In conclusion it can be said that Scotland is in a good position to face the future because the framework for action is potentially more effective than in the rest of the UK. I use the word 'potentially' advisedly because we will not succeed unless decision-makers are prepared to acknowledge some of the mistakes made in recent years, and they will also have to be very sensitive to some of the altered circumstances such as those outlined above if we are to act *before* rather than *after* events. Provided we have active public participation and a greater interest in the affairs of Government, combined with a sound understanding of the decision-making process governing the built environment, I am confident that the shape of things to come will reflect the aspirations and needs of future generations of Scots.

Notes

1. The Scottish Tourism and Recreation Planning Studies (STARPS) demonstrate that the agencies can both act together and achieve results more quickly than is normally the case in policy initiatives by central departments. In 1975 four agencies jointly decided that it would be desirable for the new regional councils to prepare strategies for sport, outdoor recreation and tourism. Coordinated action in these fields had not been required before, and by the middle of 1976 the agencies had produced two documents for the local authorities: first 'Strategic Issues' representing a corporate statement of their policies, and second a 'Guide to the Preparation of Initial Regional Strategies'. The timing compares favourably with, say, the introduction of new development plans which were worked on by central departments from 1965 until well into the 1970s.
2. Central Office of Information, Scotland, HMSO, London, 1974, pp. 12-17.
3. C. Buchanan, *Traffic in Towns: a Study of the Long Term Problems of Traffic in Urban Areas* (The Buchanan Report), Ministry of Transport, HMSO, London, 1963. National land use policy in response to the expected increase in population is not particularly well documented, but some information, including the situation in Scotland, can be found in: A. Goss, 'Some Lessons from the Humberside and Severnside Feasibility Studies,' in *Journal of the Royal Town Planning Institute,* No. 4 (April, 1972), vol. 58, pp. 167-171.
4. F.J. Osborne and A. Whittick, *The New Towns*, Leonard Hill, London, 1969.
5. Figures prepared by the Scottish Information Office and the Government Stat-

istical Service (Scottish Office), Edinburgh, 1975.

6. R.H. Matthew and P.E.A. Johnson-Marshall, *The Lothian Regional Survey and Plan,* HMSO, Edinburgh, 1966, vol. 2.

7. Office of Population Censuses and Surveys, *Population Projections 1974-2014,* Government Statistical Service, HMSO, London, 1976.

8. A.W. Hendry, *Road and Rail: an Alternative Transport Strategy for Edinburgh,* Edinburgh Amenity and Transport Association, Edinburgh, 1973.

9. P. Hall, *Urban and Regional Planning,* Penguin Books, Harmondsworth, Middlesex, 1974, pp. 230-234.

10. D.N. Skinner, *A Situation Report on Green Belts in Scotland,* Countryside Commission for Scotland, Perth, 1976.

11. J. Smith, 'Storm ahead on Ben Lomond power giant,' in the *Scotsman*, 9 August, 1976, p. 1.

12. G. Dean, 'Wind-power in West is "fantastic",' in the *Scotsman,* 15 October 1976, p. 10.

12 SCOTLAND'S DEFENCE

John Erickson

> This (Highland) spirit finds its freest scope in the life of a soldier.
> In that career, also, the instincts and traditions of his race meet
> with their fullest realisation. And thus it has come that for more
> than a century and a half, the British Army has had no braver or
> more loyal body of men than those Highland Regiments. On many
> a hard-fought field, in all parts of the world, wherever deeds of
> heroism had to be done, the pibroch has thrilled and the tartan
> has waved in the front.
>
> Sir A. Geikie, *Scottish Reminiscences*

If only it were as simple as that, the defence issue reduced to the ringing
refrain of all men 'soldiers of the Queen, m'boys', with nothing to be
said or sung, as the case may be. Myths, however, fade and even come
under direct attack—witness that most recent letter of G. Doward of
Jedburgh (printed in The *Scotsman* of 19 January 1977) which assails
'the fiction' of the prowess of the Highlander in battle and bewails the
fact that Lowlander has become almost synonymous with 'English'.
Only after '45 with the formation of the Scottish regiments, was Highland fervour blended with 'the Lowlanders skill, knowledge and deter-
mination': only then did Scottish regiments become a 'feared fighting
force'. The 51st Highland Division, the 'Highway Decorators' of inimit-
able style, was made up of men from the length and breadth of Scotland and as Mr Doward adds in all fairness not a few Englishmen. In
this quizzical, quaint fashion, much of the passion and patriotism associated with 'defence' is brought to the surface: come Highlander or Lowlander (*pace* Mr Doward), Scotland has played a prominent and consistent role in the military enterprises of the United Kingdom and 'military
nation' is still a living entity in Scotland. Sentiment apart, there is grim
reality behind much of this: witness John Prebble's brilliant and incis-
ive historical work, which pays no concessions to tawdry tales or Kipling-
esque attitudes.

We stand at a curious cross-roads, one of between nostalgia and modern military technology—the pibroch and tartan co-exist, so does the
Polaris submarine slide out of Faslane, the radars poke out from Buchan
and the RAF *Phantoms* leap from Leuchars. Perhaps the dominant
factor now is not tradition or military prowess, in the sense of military

153

brawn, but geography and the 'strategic environment', an abstraction
which hides a multitude of perils. And so to another paradox. For all
the noisesomeness of sentimentality and the verbosity of nostalgia,
'defence' in its technical context has been left largely and deliberately
unnoticed. Even more important, it is intended that it should go unnoticed. In the several feverish discussions of Scotland and its possible
future, 'defence and foreign policy' drift quite casually by, they trip off
the tongue of many, but it is not meant to be heard. To put it another
way, separatism does not quite seem to be fully separate, when defence,
the waging of war and the making of peace is to be left to Westminster.
What else determines the true viability of a nation, that it should decide
upon its fate in terms of fundamental issues of survival? It is no answer
to say that Scotland in independent form would have no enemies. No
government can abolish the 'strategic environment' at will and that
environment, even in its present form, projects quite a fearsome shadow.

In general terms the United Kingdom, of which Scotland is at the
moment an integral part, remains one of the world's major
military powers in terms of expenditure, coming sixth after the United
States, the Soviet Union, West Germany, China and France. Within this
integrated arrangement, Scotland occupies a key position, not least for
geographic reasons, an importance which extends to the defence structure
of the United Kingdom and NATO at large. The Royal Navy and the
Royal Air Force are deployed throughout Scotland; the submarine base
on the Clyde houses Polaris submarines and is thus the home of the
'national deterrent'; Holy Loch contains the United States presence and
more nuclear missile submarines; Machrihanish and Stornoway accommodate vital forward operating airfields; radar early-warning and fighter
interceptor units are sited on the east coast, itself much attended by
Soviet long-range reconnaissance aircraft; South Uist and Benbecula
furnish missile test firing ranges and the inner sound of Rassay an Underwater Testing and Evaluation Centre.

Above all, for UK-patriot, devolutionist and ardent separatist alike,
this same Scotland sticks out (if I may be allowed this ungainly phrase)
in the direction of the strategically vital UK-Iceland gap; a gap into
which the great and growing Soviet Northern Fleet obtrudes ever more
frequently and in increasing strength. Scotland, like much of the northern maritime theatre, now lies *behind* the Soviet defensive perimeter and
has done so for some time. Radar based in Scotland peers out into the
North Sea, across to the Soviet northern naval and air bases and into the
Atlantic, thus forming a spectral but formidable front line of a special
type from Saxa Vord in Shetland and Benbecula, with a main radar

station for the defence of the United Kingdom at Buchan and all augmented by the *Nimrods* flying out of Lossiemouth and the interceptor units at Leuchars; long-range maritime patrols are controlled from Pitreavie, Joint Maritime HQ for both the United Kingdom and NATO. In addition, there is a singular 'defence commitment' with the advent of off-shore resources—oil—which must be secured and guarded in one form or another.

It needs no further demonstration to assert that the place of Scotland within the UK defence system and within NATO is of major significance and likely to grow apace as the northern strategic theatre expands in importance, if only because of the impress of Soviet naval power. The Soviet Northern Fleet is the most powerful Soviet naval concentration available to the Soviet command: its units cruise the Scottish seas and its maritime reconnaissance aircraft probe Scottish skies. Let us also add the Baltic Fleet, whose newly appointed C-in-C last year made a full reconnaissance of the off-shore oil installations in a fleet exercise all his own. If Scotland *qua* Scotland has no enemies, then it has at least nosy intruders, who can even on peaceful and peacetime missions entangle themselves in oil rigs and insert themselves into communications systems.

Thus, from the heroic we come to the mundane (or the arcane, if one includes the new electronic warfare techniques, surveillance systems and continuous reconnaissance). Defence assumes a dual aspect: one dramatic with all its strategic connotations—Polaris submarines, the 'national deterrent' and the like; and the other, routine and less exciting, involving the surveillance and securing of sea and air space, but nevertheless demanding of men, resources and money. Those who search for separatism and independence might bear this in mind, that they cannot carve up radar beams or decide on 'independence' for air traffic control (not to mention air-sea rescue). It is readily apparent that Scotland is deeply enmeshed in the strategic relationships and military-political relationships of the entire northern theatre and that the significance of this relationship can only grow throughout the next decade. The 'defence map', if that can be so distinguished and identified, can only become more complex, whatever the turn of political fortunes.

At the root of the matter is the lack of general investigation of 'defence'—much is left to either rhetoric or to guesswork. It is readily understandable that under conditions of general UK integration, H. M. Government has little or no interest in enlarging on these facts and their implications, while the SNP has been similarly coy about the 'defence' ramifications of an independent Scotland. Ironically, the issue of defence is fundamental to both cases: it is the *absolute* of integration and independence alike. It could assume also a rather more sinister significance if we were to move to separation 'through conflict, acrimony and disharmony' (to use the phraseology of Mr Norman Buchan's letter to *The Times*). If separation could be 'harmoniously achieved'—and if there could be a guarantee of that—then, of course, the relevance of 'defence' would sensibly diminish. But where is there such a guarantee?

Let us look a little more closely therefore at this 'share' of Scotland in defence activity. What is interesting here is the calculation of a 'share' in terms of UK activity at large and what might be regarded as an equitable share for Scotland in terms of defence-related employment. Dr Gavin Kennedy with some considerable virtuosity has established that nine per cent is an acceptable figure for Scotland's 'share' of UK defence spending some ten per cent of domiciled Scots serve with the Armed Forces, the number of men stationed in Scotland is in the order of 17,600 (half in the Royal Navy, a quarter in the Royal Air Force), which supplies a 'net export' figure of some 19,000 men from Scotland for the Services at large. Civilian MoD employment is in the region of 22,700, representing approximately 7.8 per cent of this labour force as a whole (and, therefore, below the equity scale). Defence contractor employment involves about 13,000 men and here is unmistakable complication of the degree to which Scotland properly 'shares' in defence contract work throughout the United Kingdom. Foreign military personnel (principally American) amount to 2,400 and bring limited employment in their wake.

This in broad terms is the present scope and scale of the 'UK-integrated' defence arrangement. In so far that it can be accurately determined, Scotland falls rather below the 'equity line' (if we equate contribution to benefit, both direct and indirect) while within Scotland itself there are distinctive configurations of employment and distribution of work. This has to be the first model, namely, the present UK-integrated defence arrangement. It is sensible to assume that there is little chance of change in this overall scheme of things, even allowing for Scotland's enhanced strategic importance. Here is the 'full integration model' and it is likely to endure in this form (save for marginal adjustments to RAF *Nimrod* strength and the class of off-shore oil protection patrol ships, two of which will shortly be in service).

The second model inevitably involves devolution—but how does one 'devolve' defence? The major arrangements, in line with the full integration model, must remain largely undisturbed. Much depends on what a future Scottish Assembly might demand, possibly in terms of fishery protection (operating presently under the Ministry of Agriculture and Fisheries for Scotland, with its six ships, three of them capable of deep water patrols)—plus a special oil rig protection squadron, connected in turn with a general environmental control and policing force. Perhaps the only distinctive step which might be envisaged would involve some 'Northern environmental command' with its own 'Supremo'. It cannot be denied that multiple user interest in the North Sea must impel closer examination of hazards and environmental dangers. Much as our imagination is (or is not) seized by oil, the North Sea presents a complex intertwining of surface and sub-surface activity, maritime 'spaghetti junctions' with the underwater ribbing of oil pipelines, the massive structures of rigs and platforms, the gyrations of Post Office cables, trawls and sundry items of variegated equipment making up a truly monsterish tangle. There is an urgent demand to update and intensify hydrographic and survey work, to which the Assembly might bend its collective mind.

Will the Assembly press for greater funds for the Hydrographer to the Navy and request that this work be diverted from being a direct charge upon the Defence vote? The Assembly should in any event pay close attention to the traffic of supertankers and the VLCCs (Very Large Crude Carriers), which themselves make the updating of charts a matter of some urgency, utilising sonar techniques and charting to a greater depth, as well as ensuring the more accurate location of wrecks. As for a very thorough survey of the Continental Shelf, it could be that funding from the Defence vote will no longer suffice, so that the requisite ships and equipment must come from several parties, going far beyond the present cooperation of the Ministry of Defence and the Department of Energy.

It could be that recent Norwegian proposals for the defence and protection of 'fishing and petroleum activities' could serve as an instructive model (Table 1). If Norwegian models can serve the SNP arguments for separatism, I do not see why they should not apply to some form of devolution. The Norwegian plan envisages an expanded Coast Guard employing maritime aircraft and large helicopter carrying ships which will also incorporate fire-fighting and anti-pollution equipment, not to mention a decompression chamber for divers (with ships displacing some 2,000 tons with a patrol speed of 15 knots but with a *dash speed* of 25-27 knots). In any event, the Assembly will have to think about an 'effective protection fleet'. Bit by bit defence creeps into the debate on devolution, though it must be said that it has been accompanied largely by vulgar Parliamentary knock-about verbal antics, such as jibes about a Gadderene rush to separatism which would bring

Table 1: Protection of Off-Shore Installations: supervising the Continental Shelf

---

UK and Norwegian forces and plans compared

UK	NORWAY
Oil-rig patrol HMS *Reward* (Sunk)	(As of report of June 1975: MOD recommendations)
HMS *Jura* (P296) 1,285 tons full load: 195.3 metres overall length 2 British Polar SP 112VS-F Diesel engines, single shaft, 17 knots: Crew: 28. Equipped with 1 40-mm gun. (Leased to Ministry of Defence: commissioned 1973)	Expansion of Naval Fisheries Protection Service and turned into a Coast Guard: relying on combined use of maritime aircraft and larger, helicopter-carrying ships. Ships to be equipped with helo-platforms and hangars: also to carry equipment for combating oil pollution and fire-fighting equipment, also to be equipped with decompression chamber.
Patrol ships (class of 5) specifications: 195 ft. overall length 1,300 tonnes d. Fuel capacity: 275 tonnes Speed: 16 knots	Proposals for ship design: displacement: 2,000 tons Patrol speed: 15 knots, but 'dash' speed of 25-27 knots:
Endurance: 7,000 nm at 12 knots, 21 days patrol endurance.	Fleet number: 10 ships, with 7 acquired in first instance, with 3 existing survey ships to be used (modernised, updated electronics)
Armament: 1 40-mm Bofors gun.	1 specialised ship for handling saturation diving, able to operate submarine vessels for inspection down to 500 metres.
Crew: 5 officers, 29 ratings, plus emergency accommodation for further 25 men up to 5 days.	Crewing: 20 per cent relief crews to each ship above normal complement.
Carries pollution dispersal equipment: 2 Gemini dinghies. No ship-borne helicopter, (One vessel commissioned)	Helicopters: One squadron attached to these ships (6 helicopters) plus one helicopter in Stavanger area.
Aircraft: Proposed modification of up to 4 RAF aircraft: patrolling meanwhile by aircraft of Strike and Training Command.	Aircraft: 3 Orion maritime patrol aircraft —to provide twice-weekly survey in each and every year.
	Special unit: Formed from Navy (Marine Commandoes) and Parachute Commandos (Army) for 'catastrophe' accidents, sabotage, high-jacking, terrorism.

the grand climacteric of 'a Scottish Navy in Troon Harbour'. It was left to Mr Tam Dalyell to ask in very sensible terms what would be the defence implications if UK-integration were put at risk. What would be the cost of a separate Scottish, Army, Navy and Air Force?

Like the model of full UK-integration, the devolution model leaves little room for manoeuvre or change, unless a Scottish Assembly grasps the environmental/protection thorn in full. Another possible issue for greater 'devolved' control could be civilian employment by the Ministry of Defence. The present government has committed itself to the transfer of several thousand Ministry of Defence jobs to the Glasgow area in the 1980s, which would continue to maintain this element of 'equity' in terms of Scotland's 'share' of employment, everything else being equal. Nor can Scotland's important military-industrial base be forgotten, whether this be counted as separate industrial establishments (such as the Clyde submarine base itself, or Rosyth Naval Dockyard) or major and highly specialised firms such as Yarrow and naval construction or Ferranti and electronics. Certainly, some aspects of this picture could change with further modification in and contraction of the United Kingdom's defence activities.

The future of the British sea-based deterrent (the Polaris submarine force) will clearly come to the fore in the next decade (as indeed it might become the focus of more immediate attention with the advent of the Carter Administration in the United States), while the possible coalescence of the Polaris force based in Devonport with the retention of Chatham's dockyard facilities could obviously affect the future of Rosyth. The five nuclear berths which could become available in the Devonport-Chatham area will, according to Ministry of Defence assurances, readily suffice to serve the Polaris force and afford that extra advantage of permitting the disarming, refitting and re-arming of the boats all in one locality (as opposed to the cycle of disarming in the Clyde, refitting at Rosyth and then rearming in the Clyde). Removal of this source of employment would affect jobs on some considerable scale, while we must wait and see what, if any, counterbalance would be provided by the transfer of other jobs to the Glasgow area.

I have argued, I hope with some justification, that neither the UK-integrated model nor the devolution model can appreciably affect the arrangement of defence matters in the Scottish context. The devolution of defence is scarcely credible, save for some great control over environmental supervision where military resources (manpower, as well as command and control facilities) are required and for some attention to the problems of defence-related employment in Scotland. But rather than jumping at once from the devolution model to a consideration of defence under conditions of total separation, I should like to interpose what might best be described as the 'disappointed devolution' state of affairs, a condition which might conceivably induce treading what Sir Andrew Gilchrist has called 'unconstitutional paths'. This could give the 'defence issue' an ugly twist, bringing both para-military and pseudo-military elements (a distinction which I believe to be important in registering the profiles and organisational patterns of activist groups) into play. The point was well made by *The 1320 Club* at the beginning of 1976 with a warning that any delay in producing 'effective devolution' could result in 'the possibility of civil disorder'. It is easy, of course, to be alarmist but it is equally facile to be totally complacent.

Here it is necessary to take a step which marks a deliberate suspension of belief, namely, to assume that there has been a constitutional transition to a status embodying an independent Scottish state and thence an independent military establishment. Understandably enough, the SNP starts from the accomplished fact, the deed, of separate status and can thus ignore all the technicalities of disentangling an integrated defence establishment—witness the agonies and absurdities of the Indo-Pakistan *caesura* of 1946-47—and, by the same token, must take little or no account of internal security problems during the transitional phase. That is precisely what I mean by a suspension of belief, for such it must surely be in large part, though Mr William Wolfe (Chairman of the SNP) in his statement on SNP defence policy in November 1976, referred to a 'joint command' designed and designated to function during this same period which he envisaged might last for some three years before independent Scottish forces came fully into existence. This leaps the hurdle of transition (metaphysically at least), but it is avowedly vague: 'joint services' for defence among UK countries are to operate for a limited period and will be subject to the approval of the Scottish Parliament, but again this is virtually devoid of meaning and operational significance. Much must also wait on the 'real situation' which will prevail after the declaration of independence and on the decisions of a Scottish Parliament.

13 THE POLITICAL RESPONSE

James Kellas

Political power determines the allocation of resources, and even the values, of society. It will determine what new system of government, if any, is to be introduced in Scotland in the future. But it is not an easy thing to analyse, since it can derive from many different sources—votes in elections, economic strength, or brute force. Moreover, in the case of political power in Scotland, there is difficulty in saying how much power is derived from Scotland and how much is derived from London, from Brussels, or from the United States.

To add further to the problem, it is necessary here to distinguish between power *now* and power *in the future*. 'Political change' has recently been analysed for Britain as a whole,[1] and the chief characteristic has been the differences between 'political generations'. One of the few safe predictions in society and politics is that the same people will not be running the country fifty years from now. It is also clear that lifestyles and expectations change from one generation to another. Politics and the exercise of political power reflect, as well as shape, the more general changes which come about through scientific, technological, educational, medical, economic and cultural development. Politics represent a complexity of inter-relationships, not only with other segments of life, but between power in Scotland and power wielded elsewhere.

One starts perhaps with an emotional, or at least pre-conceived, attitude towards the subject. The contributors to this book are broadly 'pessimists' or 'optimists' about the future of Scotland. Professor Smout believes that devolution points in the direction of 'political stalemate', when 'the crazy terrorist reaches for his gun'. Professor Erickson warns of civil unrest and violence in an independent Scotland. Others, myself included, welcome the prospect of political change and Scottish self-government as providing new opportunities, as well as being consistent with the other developments in Scottish life. Naturally, each school of thought can marshall evidence from past, present and even future to support its stance. But nothing can be 'proved', and it is almost impossible to make converts. Even the passage of time rarely alters such basic attitudes. Scotland joined England in 1707, and Marx wrote the Communist Manifesto in 1848, yet Scottish nationalists and communists are

161

still much the same today, in their basic ideas.

These are 'men of action', dedicated towards achieving political ends, while 'political scientists' seek a correct analysis of political forces, even if they too have attitudes and pre-conceptions. My study of the *Scottish Political System*[2] leads me to believe in the essential harmony of that system with the British political system as a whole. This is not because it is subservient in some way, or essentially powerless, but because the unity of the United Kingdom has always been consistent with a fair amount of diversity between the different parts of the country. In the case of Scotland, separate legal, legislative, administrative, educational and ecclesiastical systems co-exist with those of England. While the British Government and Parliament have formal sovereignty over the whole of Britain, neither has successfully exercised its legal powers without the broad consent of the different social and territorial groups in the country. One of the reasons for Mr Heath's defeat in February 1974 was that he offended against the predominant view that government should be by consensus. In another context, the isolation of Northern Ireland from British politics after 1920, and until 1968, was the result of the feeling in Great Britain that the Ulstermen should be left to sort out their own problems. The intervention of London into Ulster politics after 1968 was an exception to the rule, albeit inevitable when Ulster lost the ability to control its own affairs.

The point about Scotland is that London rule is indeed British rule, not English rule, because it is rarely imposed on an unwilling Scotland. London takes a great deal of trouble to avoid breaking the territorial consensus which prevails in the United Kingdom. In return, Scotland rarely rebels against a decision of the British Government and Parliament, and if it does, there is usually an accommodation to suit the Scots. The threat from the Industry minister Mr Varley, in 1975, that he would let Chrysler close in Scotland, was overruled in Cabinet by Mr Ross, Secretary of State for Scotland, with the support of the Prime Minister and other members of the Cabinet. Another Scottish-English conflict was over the introduction of Summer Time (renamed 'British Standard Time') from October 1968 to October 1971. Of course, the winter mornings in Scotland were much darker than in England, and Scottish opinion hardened against the new Time. The House of Commons heeded the opinion of Scottish MPs of all parties, and on December 2nd 1970 voted to end BST for the following winter. Again, the White Paper on devolution (November 1975) was attacked in Scotland as not going far enough. By August 1976 a supplementary White Paper was issued which gave more powers to the Scottish Assembly, despite the misgivings of many English MPs.

Thus British governments, of whatever party, govern according to the wishes of the electorate and the predominant interests in the country. One of these interests is Scotland, another the trade union movement, a third the business community. While there are marked differences in emphasis between Labour and Conservative governments in policy, each is constrained at the end of the day by the political power represented by the voters and the organised interest groups. It is this which explains the coming together of the parties' policies on socio-economic matters, and the give-and-take on such questions as devolution to Scotland and Wales.

I believe this to be a general truth about British politics, but it should not disguise the fact that politics rarely means 'fair shares for all'. Power is unequally distributed, partly because wealth is unequally distributed, but also because territorial and electoral pressures impinge on governments in an uneven fashion. It is in the latter respect that Scotland has shown its power lately, for by voting Nationalist the Scottish electorate has exercised a most potent leverage on the central authorities, out of proportion to its population, size, or economic wealth.

Political scientists find it more difficult to relate territory to power than such indicators as social class. In Britain, it was said in 1967 by one political scientist, 'Class is the basis of British party politics; all else is embellishment and detail.'[3] In this theory, Scotland does not divide from England, but the working class throughout the country divides from the middle class; hence the Labour and Conservative party dominance. And Scotland then seemed to bear this out: Labour and Conservative together got 88 per cent of the vote in 1966 in Scotland, with the Liberals at seven per cent and the SNP at five per cent.

But in the middle 1970s, the electoral aspects of politics have been transformed. The Labour and Conservative vote in Scotland combined has dropped to 61 per cent in the general election of October 1974, with the SNP 30.4 per cent and the Liberals 8.3 per cent. With the SNP now getting as many votes as the 'class parties' in Scotland, territory has become a strong rival to class in the minds of many Scottish voters, and the SNP itself is made up of supporters fairly evenly spread throughout the social classes.[4] Something the same has happened in England too, with increased Liberal voting, but there the 'territorial dimension' is hardly present at all. This dimension is ambiguous, however, even in Scotland. For while the SNP wants Scotland to be an independent country, the opinion polls indicate that only around one-fifth of the Scottish electorate agree, and that this proportion has not changed much over the years. Even the numbers wanting devolution have not altered greatly, though it is certainly true that the kind of devolution that is asked for in the mid-1970s is more akin to federalism than were the devolution proposals of the past. In particular, power over the Scottish economy and over oil revenues is an added dimension of home rule demands today. Compared with the past too, there is more intensity in the discussion of devolution in Scotland: more newspapers support it, and give it prominence, there is more broadcasting devoted to it, and the parties and pressure groups have to give it full attention. While this is obviously connected with the voting for the SNP and the threat to the seats held by the major parties, it may also be due to fundamental changes in Scottish life, leading to a reappraisal of Scotland's position in the United Kingdom.

The first change relates to the population and social structure of Scotland. It is of course notorious that Scotland has lost large numbers of its people through emigration. During the 1960s alone there was a net loss through migration of 338,000 people, and the natural increase of the population just kept the total population steady. The effect of this on political power is interesting to consider. If it is true that the more skilled, educated and ambitious people tend to emigrate, because there is a demand for their abilities elsewhere, then Scotland suffered through the loss of a particularly important section of society in political terms. For political activists tend to be drawn from such people, as do industrial innovators. In party political terms, one suspects that the Conservative Party may have suffered badly through the loss of this type of person, who simply left Scotland altogether.

The political class or 'establishment' in Scotland at the close of the 1960s was thus a shrinking group of middle class, skilled or highly educated people, who could be found in the key professions of the historic Scotland—the law, education, church, central and local government and medicine, but to a lesser extent in industry and the trade unions. This class is not only Conservative in politics, although it has a tendency to be so. It also provides the other parties with their MPs and councillors, and the trade unions with their leaders. The fact that this class was shrinking in Scotland in the 1960s contributed to an over-dependence on the London Establishment, and the ability to take decisions in Scotland itself diminished in proportion to the exodus of the most able people.

By the early 1970s, however, the net emigration from Scotland was dropping sharply, and a fair number of able people returned, to exploit the oil in the North Sea, take jobs in new industries, and to swell the ranks of public administration. At the same time, the younger generation tended to stay in Scotland rather than to leave, as job prospects grew worse in England and abroad, and Scotland's relative employment position improved. It is this new generation of Scots and immigrants to Scotland which holds the key to the future of Scotland, and which is quite distinct in many ways from the older generation. In electoral terms, political generations form their voting habits when young and tend to remain true to the party preferences of their youth.[5] Thus the 'generation' of Stanley Baldwin is predominantly Conservative, and the 'generation' of Clement Attlee predominantly Labour. There seems little doubt the 'generation' of George Reid (SNP MP for Clackmannan and East Stirlingshire) and Jim Sillars (Scottish Labour MP for South Ayrshire) is predominantly nationalist, and impatient with 'British' institutions.

As well as the changing population, there is the changing economy, which also has important effects on politics. The decline of the older industries such as mining, heavy engineering and agriculture, has affected the political scene, not only through the resulting unemployment and its associated discontents, but also because it has weakened some of the traditional bases of the political parties. The SNP was able to gain Hamilton in 1967, and Clackmannan and East Stirlingshire in 1974, partly because the strength of the Labour Party in the mining constituencies had been sapped by the closure of the mines. Conversely, the development of new industries of a modern technological nature in the new towns such as Cumbernauld and East Kilbride, and in places like Falkirk, has been associated with a specially strong vote for the SNP. Another stronghold for the Nationalists is the area affected by North Sea oil developments, which stretches from Dundee northwards to Shetland. Much of this area was already fertile ground for minor parties before oil, since rural communities are much less bound by class politics than are industrialised ones.

Wherever new towns, new industries, and small, classless communities are to be found, or where the old working class has been decimated or demoralised through industrial change or years of neglect (Govan is an example of the latter category, and it was held by the SNP from November 1973 to February 1974), there the SNP has made striking advances. This means that both 'relative affluence' and 'relative deprivation' can break down voting loyalties, but in either case the voters must be impressed by the failure of the major parties to better their conditions, and by the credibility of using a Nationalist vote to get things moving.

These are the underlying signs of change in Scottish society and politics. But how does the present political élite behave, and what are the signs of a new political élite emerging? Whether one adopts the Marxist analysis of a 'ruling class', or the concept of a 'ruling élite', or 'Establishment', or just 'government', it is difficult to identify these people in a Scottish context. Marxists base political power on the ownership of the means of production, but since so much Scottish industry is in non-Scottish hands, this analysis makes the ruling class in Scotland partly a non-Scottish class — whether based in London or in the USA. Nevertheless some sociologists have written about a Scottish ruling class, chiefly industrialists, bankers, and insurance men, who between them tie up most of the financial power of Scotland.[6]

In a Marxist interpretation, these people also constitute the political rulers of Scotland. But there is an obvious snag here in that the ostensible government in Scotland is often Labour, whether as a result of Labour control at Westminster, or Labour control at local government level. Marxists get round this by saying that these party labels make no difference to real political power, which remains vested in the capitalist class as long as the economic system is capitalist.

The alternative, 'élite' analysis is also ambiguous as far as Scotland is concerned. One can think of a Scottish Establishment as comprising those in positions of political, social and economic power. But the British Establishment includes some of the Scottish Establishment. The Secretary of State for Scotland, for example, is in both the British and Scottish Establishments, as is Mr Hugh Fraser, now a member of the SNP and owner of many commercial establishments in Scotland and in London. But the Moderator of the General Assembly of the Church of Scotland seems to operate almost entirely within the Scottish context, and Mr James Milne, General Secretary of the STUC, defers to Mr Len Murray, of the TUC, in the 'social contract' negotiations with the government. Mr Milne, however, is a force to be reckoned with in Scotland itself.

One can avoid the 'ruling class' and 'ruling élite' methods of analysing power by using a 'decision-making' or 'case-study' approach. This tackles the outcomes of politics, the decisions, and traces those responsible for making them. The Scottish political system is a decision-making system, because it allows Scots to take decisions in Scotland. It also allows them to feed in proposals to the British political system, which takes decisions at central level in London, and also to the EEC system, which decides matters at Brussels. In a purely formal analysis, only the British and European bodies have decision-making powers, and there are no independent Scottish decision-makers. Even the Scottish courts are ultimately subject to the sovereignty of Parliament, although it says in the Treaty of Union that the independence of the Scottish courts is guaranteed for all time.

In practice a large number of people in Scotland are engaged in taking decisions, some important politically, and others of a more routine nature. For example, Scottish party conferences decide policy on devolution, and Scottish Office officials approve the plans for a local school submitted by a local authority. A decision was made to change the licensing laws, after prolonged debate and pressure, and the decision by Glasgow Corporation to allow public houses in their housing estates. A great number of Scottish political decisions are taken under the shadow of, or actually inside, the Scottish Office in Edinburgh. The ministers and civil servants of St Andrew's House run Scotland in as centralised and as efficient a manner as Whitehall runs Britain. Clearly, a focus for the Scottish ruling élite is to be found in the corridors of St Andrew's House and a constant stream of councillors, officials, pressure group deputations and individual citizens converge there to seek a favourable decision for their cause.

This is a variant of the 'corporate state', because it operates without any democratically-elected Scottish body. The interest groups meet with the civil servants and ministers in St Andrew's House and they decide between them what is to be done. This is, for example, how most educational policy is arrived at. Bodies such as the Scottish Teachers' Salaries Committee and the Scottish Teachers' Service Conditions Committee negotiate contracts between the teachers' organisations and the government and local authorities, but Parliament and the public know little of how these bodies operate and how their members are chosen. There is no public forum for educational policy-making in Scotland, and Parliament spends barely three or four hours a year on the subject.

The Secretary of State retains a vast patronage over public bodies in Scotland, and the new political class or generation is unlikely to be included in the nominations. Even the judiciary is linked to political patronage in Scotland. The established pressure groups, ranging from the trade unions and professional associations to the local authorities and their association, are also representative of the older political class, and have been integrated to the corporate state through their vested rights of representation on the many public bodies on the land. There is thus some way to go before the established order in Scotland gives way to the new.

The number of decisions which can fall within the power of the Scottish political system is limited by the fact that Scotland is not an independent country. There is a great deal of reference to London, involving the old political class in continual travelling, telex communication, and letter-writing. It is said that on the platforms of Waverley Station, Edinburgh, ministers going south to answer parliamentary questions in London cross with their civil servants coming back from Whitehall to look up the files in Edinburgh for the answers. While this is certainly good for British Rail, it does nothing for efficient public administration.

Under the conditions of official secrecy it is impossible to know how much 'checking-out' there has to be between Edinburgh and London before anything can be decided. And after that, how much freedom the Scots have to go their own way is not clear. One can only judge by results, by the decisions themselves. These point rather ambiguously to numerous differences in Scottish as opposed to English decisions, and to Scottish 'privileges' within the UK, but also to notorious 'blockages' in the legislative process at Westminster, and 'multiple deprivation' in the most heavily populated areas of Scotland.[7] Some decisions clearly have come about because the Scottish political class or élite decided that they should come about, and then operated the British and Scottish political systems to bring them about. Well-known examples are most moral, legal, and educational matters which do not involve a 'Treasury' decision. But it must also be said that blockages at Westminster have prevented legislation in these areas too, and that legislation covering Scotland has sometimes paid scant attention to the wishes of the Scottish élite. As Lord Hunter, Chairman of the Scottish Law Commission, said in 1975,

> There were difficulties in getting the Scottish viewpoint across in England, and in some cases Scotland had no representation on certain committees where UK legislation affected Scotland. The statutory Scotsman on a committee is in a very difficult position. You have to be very determined to get the Scottish view across to them. The thinking is different.[8]

These difficulties are now compounded by British entry to the European Community, for even the 'statutory Scotsman' may not be present in the British delegation to Brussels, and the Scottish case can go by default.[9]

It might be thought that the Scottish Office would be well placed to put the Scottish case in Whitehall, and it certainly likes to think of itself as a Whitehall department, not an Edinburgh one. Senior civil servants in St Andrew's House believe that they are helping to shape UK policy rather than producing a separate Scottish policy. But their efforts at shaping economic policy have proved long and painful. Under the Conservatives (1970-74), a valiant attempt was made by Edinburgh to seize the initiative on North Sea Oil policy, and Lord Polwarth was appointed Minister of State for the purpose. But Whitehall was too strong for it, and the Department of Energy and the Department of Industry kept control. Sir William McEwan Younger, the industrialist and former chairman of the Scottish Conservatives, publicly attacked Whitehall for 'having displayed in matters relating to off-shore oil a mixture of ignorance and arrogance which demonstrated over-centralisation at its worst'.[10] And Lord Hunter confirmed that in the Department of Industry Scotland was a still, small voice when legislation affecting Scots private law was contemplated.[11]

These are obviously unhappy men of the Scottish Establishment within the present Union, but it should not be thought that judges and industrialists on the whole are actively seeking devolution. Rather the reverse. The judges of the Court of Session have collectively pronounced their opposition to being themselves devolved to the control of a Scottish Assembly, and the CBI, with the Chambers of Commerce, dislikes the devolution proposals. So too do many civil servants in the Scottish Office, and many university teachers in Scotland. It is not from these men, therefore, that the new political class in Scotland is to be drawn, unless they undergo rapid conversion to new ways of life. Who then are the new people of politics in Scotland, and what are they likely to make of the future of Scotland?

I turn first to the younger generation. All our information about the political views of the young people of Scotland tells us that they have moved furthest from the major 'class' parties towards the SNP and the Liberals. In some surveys almost half of those under 35 said they would support the SNP.[12] All the surveys show that older people vote predominantly for the major parties. If the current theory of 'political change in Britain' (see note 1) is correct, and the younger generation remains true to its early allegiances, then the major parties are in trouble for some time to come, and may eventually be reduced to minor status. The advent of the Scottish Labour Party in December 1975 is another indication of the new political class asserting itself. Jim Sillars has attracted many young people away from the Labour Party, and some of the SNP, and he does not disguise his contempt for, and impatience with, the old order in Scotland and in the UK generally. However successful or otherwise he may be in electoral terms in the short term, he represents a completely different image from the Labour Party of the now-retired Willie Ross (Secretary of State for Scotland, 1964-70, 1974-76).

It may be said that youth is a pretty insecure basis on which to base political power. The younger generation is often apathetic, unwilling to sustain political activity over a period, and alienated from the 'real' world of politics, where wheeling and dealing and routine public administration must apparently prevail. And there is no doubt that the old political class remains in charge largely because it is prepared to do the work, however patronisingly and inefficiently. Will the new political class be any different? One of the snags to linking political change with generational change is that quite often the young soon come to resemble their elders, or indeed may have always done so.[13] In other words, some might say, 'the more it changes the more it is the same thing', and even if the voting preferences change, other attitudes may remain conservative.

But we have already seen pointers in the changing society and economy which, when added to changes in party support and in the structure of government lead to a more fundamental transformation in Scottish politics. To emphasise these, the sources and nature of political information in Scotland are changing rapidly. In school and university, Scotland is increasingly studied, with special reference to political, economic and social questions. In the media, there is much more attention paid to Scottish affairs, and a frankly nationalist tone pervades even the Labour and Conservative press. The development of 'investigative journalism', although weaker in Scotland than in Fleet Street, complements the educational changes in bringing to the new generation an awareness of what is going on which is salutary for democracy, and particularly good for Scotland, which, as we have seen, indulges in secretive, patronage-ridden government. Institutional changes have helped this change, with the establishment of community councils, schools councils, and other watchdog bodies. They do not, of course, live up to all expectations, but their very existence would not have been contemplated in the Scotland of the 1950s. MPs, councillors and officials have to deal with far more correspondence and public interest in decisions than ever before, and the people no longer take everything lying down. Least of all does the younger generation, as is evidenced by student demonstrations and strikes led by young teachers and shop stewards, often against the wishes of their elders. Recent industrial disputes in Scotland (e.g. Upper Clyde Shipbuilders, Chrysler, *Scottish Daily News*) show that workers do not readily accept decisions taken from a distance if these threaten their livelihood.

The signs are therefore optimistic that the future of Scotland in political terms will be a more lively and critical affair than anything we have known in Scottish politics to date. But it could also be more un-

stable, and it will certainly open up areas of conflict within Scotland
and between Scotland and England. But this should not be lamented,
and is indeed a healthy alternative to the closed consensus of established
groups which has been the norm for so long.

This is of course the 'emotional' or 'preconceived' background to the
analysis, and it is possible to construct alternative interpretations with a
less happy outcome. One of these states that if left to themselves the
Scots would divide and quarrel. Shetland has already threatened to
'leave' if devolution for Scotland is granted, and Aberdeen continually
protests at having to pay subsidies to Clydeside. Needless to say, Edinburgh fears Glasgow's numerical superiority, and Catholics are said to
dread a 'Protestant ascendancy'. The universities cling to the UK connection as a means of saving them from the supposed levelling effects of
the rest of Scottish education, and the Scottish judges complain that
their prestige would be diminished if they were linked to an Edinburgh
Assembly rather than to Westminster. There is certainly fertile ground
for the pessimists here, who might consider that UK (or English)
influences alone keep Scotland civilised.

The conclusion on that score depends partly on an assessment of
Scottish life and character, but Scotland alone will not control its own
affairs. Political power over Scotland will still be partly derived from
London and abroad, and the conflicts engendered through new systems
of government could depend as much on non-Scottish as on Scottish
attitudes and actions. In the short term, the failure of Westminster to
provide for Scottish devolution when the majority of Scottish MPs are
committed to it, and when indeed the British parties are pledged to
action, could well engender a reaction in Scotland against the Union. It
would appear that constitutional methods did not give expression to
Scottish aspirations, and that 'England' was opposed to 'Scotland'. This
could lead quickly to independence for Scotland, if the will were there.

But this would not be in keeping with the history of the Union until
now, which has demonstrated a balance of British, English and Scottish
interests with many examples of mutual compromise. On this reading,
then, no 'slippery slope to independence' or to civil war would occur,
because consensus would be re-established. It should not be thought,
however, that even Scottish independence itself would fundamentally
affect that consensus. The SNP has already shown that its concept of
an independent Scotland involves an 'Association of the British Isles',
probable membership of the European Community, and a sharing of
oil and other natural resources. It is fiercely opposed to the term 'separatism', preferring to speak of 'independence'. Beyond the statements of

the SNP, the inter-marriage of Scots with English, the close linguistic, cultural and commercial links of Scotland and England, and the shared political culture since 1707, all point to the continuing harmony of politics in Great Britain (excluding Northern Ireland, of course).

Although Scots are an argumentative and somewhat divisive nation, they are also versed in citizenship, and pragmatic, perhaps not so much as the English, but certainly more so than the Irish, the French, the Germans and the Italians. Scottish religious conflicts, for example, are largely a thing of the past, and the Glasgow Labour Party is living proof that Catholics and Protestants can work together in the same political party for agreed ends. The Moderator of the General Assembly of the Church of Scotland and the Roman Catholic Archbishop of Glasgow talk together publicly on problems of mutual concern. So I am sure would a government of Scotland and a government of England or of the United Kingdom.

There will have to be some flexing of muscles before the new political order takes over in Scotland, and there will be more conflict, of an institutional and party political nature, than before. A shake-out is needed, not only within Scotland, but between Scotland and London. It will not be a bloody revolution, but an exciting and profitable experiment in British political life. It will be especially salutary for Scotland to have 'responsible government', whether through devolution, federalism or independence. For the present political system does not match up to the changing structure of the economy and society in Scotland. It too must undergo generational change.

Notes

1. D. Butler and D. Stokes, *Political Change in Britain*, 1st ed., Macmillan, London, 1969. 2nd ed., 1975.

2. J.G. Kellas, *The Scottish Political System*, 2nd ed., Cambridge University Press, Cambridge, 1975.

3. P.G.J. Pulzer, *Political Representation and Elections in Britain*, London, Allen and Unwin, 3rd ed., 1975, p. 102.

4. See for example, Kellas, op.cit. p. 131, for survey figures.

5. Butler and Stokes, op.cit. pp. 59-64. (1st ed.)

6. J. Scott and M. Hughes, 'The Scottish Ruling Class: Problems of Analysis and Data', in A.A. MacLaren (ed.), *Social Class in Scotland: Past and Present*, John Donald, Edinburgh, 1976, pp. 166-88.

7. Scotland has most of the areas of multiple deprivation in Britain, according to an official Report, *Census Indicators of Urban Deprivation*, Department of the Environment, London, April 1975.

8. *Scotsman*, 7 March 1975.

9. See the Hansard Society's Report *The British People: Their Voice in Europe*, Teakfield, London 1977.

10. *Scotsman*, 2 November 1974.
11. *Ibid.*, 3 March 1975.
12. e.g. System Three Scotland Survey for Granada TV, *Scotsman*, 10 November 1975.
13. A survey of opinion among Scots aged between 16 and 20 showed little evidence of radicalism relating to moral and social questions. *Scotsman*, 26-29 April 1976.

14 AFTERWORD

William Robertson

Less concrete, but just as important as the other issues discussed in this book, is the purpose, or objective, towards which the community feels impelled to steer in the midst of the political confusion of events. An objective of this general kind is more than the sum of all the separate components which have been reviewed—it is something which lies deeper in the consciousness of the community—or sometimes perhaps in its subconsciousness. Earlier contributions have made clear the worldwide nature of the problem of identity, the crisis of the community. Why does this exist, and what distinctively Scottish response should there be to it?

Science, as it has developed over the last two hundred years has released a veritable explosion in our knowledge of the material world— because we have broken through the surface of visible, tangible materials and obtained access to the invisible, intangible particles and powers which we can then reassemble in a myriad fashion. This explosion of knowledge has created the eruption of invention that we call technology. In our own century the technological process has generated inventions in such number and of such magnitude as to create a discontinuity in human history. These inventions have in turn produced the unending social crises with which we live on an international scale, including World War I, a world trade depression, World War II and world problems of peace, poverty and pollution. At the political level, the social changes have in turn created demands and stresses such that most of the political systems which ran the world's affairs within living memory have collapsed or have been overthrown. These political changes have demanded new insights into the bedrock of belief in the purpose of individual existence which could make sense and provide control of turbulent events. Where old systems of religious belief could not match these demands, there emerged new views of the nature and purpose of man to supply the need.

Some of these new views have been intellectual constructs based on philosophical and economic analyses of the history of man. Such are the forms of Marxism: and since they must have the authority of truth, they are in their political form usually totalitarian. Other revolutions have looked for truth about man in other directions: the philosopher of

174

the Nazi regime, Rosenburg, in writing 'The Myth of the Twentieth Century' gave expression to a racial philosophy, reaching down to Nietzsche for roots. Others again believe hopefully that the pressure of events will somehow hammer out a new pragmatic political philosophy.

In these terms it is clear that we are not living in a world from which crises will depart: they will continue indefinitely. There is no solution. It may be a symptom of the present that a series on the Future for Scotland includes no address on religion: to quote Smout, 'Scotland is part of the West: agnostic'. In the same age that has proclaimed the death of God, many men believe that they do not themselves exist except as manifestations, not yet quite explained, on the surface of physical and chemical events. The death of God and of self seem to hang together. The complexity and insecurity of the world lead people either to opt for the short view or for systems which provide security, even at the sacrifice of some degree of liberty. Until our times, man has been afraid of the unknown: now he has more fear of knowledge.

An attempt to create an anticipation for Scotland out of its parts, but without an integrating idea or ideal would merely create greater chaos. It would recall the fate of the National Institute for Co-ordinated Experiments described in C.S. Lewis's book, *That Hideous Strength*. The University College which bids fair to take over the affairs of the country is in the end of the day defeated by the curse of the Tower of Babel. The attempt poses a choice between the ideas and the ideals. 'What is truth?', said jesting Pilate, and would not wait for an answer. It is fashionable enough to say that it should include something transcendental: that's a nice vague word. In the Scottish community the idea of human purpose has always been rooted in the belief of God acting in history. It is in that belief I stand.

At the head of King Street in Stirling, there stands a stone cupola which supports a statue of Sir William Wallace, surrounded by words like 'Liberty'. Under the cupola is the inscription, 'God in History', Psalms II, Verse 2. The modern Scotland has not been able to bring its views of material and spiritual reality so conveniently together. The explosion of knowledge of the realities of the physical world must now be matched by a corresponding expansion of the understanding of the reality of the spirit and the purpose of man if they are to embrace and contain the flow of social and political events. To illustrate the present gap, there are those—like myself—who find themselves at times joining together to think about God's purpose in the ordinary situation of life, and singing hymns such as:

Earth might be fair and all men glad and wise:
Age after age their tragic empires rise
Built while they dream and in that dreaming weep:
Would man but wake from out his haunted sleep,
Earth might be fair and all men glad and wise.

But these groups usually know little about the actualities of empires, whether political or industrial or financial, so are unable to design alarm clocks with which to wake the sleepers, let alone to tell them what the time of day is if they were to waken up.

When two years ago the institutions of Britain were at real risk they were saved by the tough fibre of institutions and of individuals, rather than by any belief-based conviction of the right course to be followed. While there are those in positions of authority who subscribe to a religious view of human reality, even they for the most part find it very difficult to establish a relationship between that view and the course of events in which they live. Between these two areas of reality—of affairs and of human spirit—bridges have to be built to span the gap. It is a fascinating and challenging prospect.

Whether or not the Christian view of human purpose prevails, it remains true that the nature of Scotland in the future will be determined not only by the necessarily modest efforts to cope one at a time with the different sectors of life as they have been set out in this series, not only by efforts to integrate them through governmental or institutional means, but also by the underlying belief of the community—or lack of it—as to the objective in whose service it sets its life. That objective will take shape, by intent or by defect. It is not only nature that abhors a vacuum—so does the human spirit, and it will be filled—the biggest question for the future of Scotland is: 'By what, or by whom?'

INDEX